MINIATURE BONSAI

春季的第一件事

並不是负担

只是栽花之乐

杏人

MINIATURE
BONSAI

Herb L. Gustafson

Sterling Publishing Co., Inc.
New York

Edited by Jeanette Green
Designed by Judy Morgan

Library of Congress Cataloging-in-Publication Data

Gustafson, Herb L.
    Miniature bonsai / by Herb L. Gustafson.
        p.   cm.
    Includes index.
    ISBN 0-8069-0982-X
    1. Bonsai.   2. Bonsai—Pictorial works.   I. Title.
SB433.5.G874   1995
635.9′772—dc20   95-18637
                                                           CIP

1   3   5   7   9   10   8   6   4   2

Published by Sterling Publishing Company, Inc.
387 Park Avenue South, New York, N.Y. 10016
© 1995 by Herb L. Gustafson
Distributed in Canada by Sterling Publishing
% Canadian Manda Group, One Atlantic Avenue, Suite 105
Toronto, Ontario, Canada M6K 3E7
Distributed in Great Britain and Europe by Cassell PLC
Wellington House, 125 Strand, London WC2R 0BB, England
Distributed in Australia by Capricorn Link (Australia) Pty Ltd.
P.O. Box 6651, Baulkham Hills, Business Centre, NSW 2153, Australia
Printed in Hong Kong
All rights reserved

Sterling ISBN 0-8069-0982-X

Acknowledgments

I would like to thank my wife, Susan Y. Gustafson, for her tireless efforts on the computer. I greatly appreciate her contribution to the production of this manuscript, her fourth to date. For their constant support and encouragement, I cannot thank my father, John M. Gustafson, and my "other parents," Lyle and Bunny Watson, enough. With such strong support, I am able to create better and better bonsai.

Thank you, Bob Baltzer, of Baltzer's Specialized Nursery, Pleasant Hill, Oregon, for allowing me to capture your Japanese maples in fall color. And I also appreciate use of plant material from The Indoor Garden, Eugene, Oregon, for some of the tropical bonsai shown here. Thank you, Greg and Sue Wilson, for allowing me to photograph plants from your nursery.

The spectacular Chinese sumi *brush paintings and Chinese lettering found in this book were rendered by Kathy Hoy. They add a wonderful historical feeling to this work. I also thank Sally A. Markos for permission to use her drawings of single tree styles of bonsai (pp. 58 to 63), originally used in my book* The Bonsai Workshop *(Sterling, 1994). Rodman Neumann has done justice to my manuscripts and been a joy to work with. I am proud to include his photograph of Hopewell Cape in chapter 2.*

A special thank-you goes out to all my students at Lane Community College. All of you can rightly feel that part of this book belongs to you. Without your questions, helpful suggestions, and participation, I could not have been stimulated to rise up to the challenge of another manuscript. To all of you, I am grateful.

Herb L. Gustafson

Contents

Preface

At first glance, the words *miniature* and *bonsai* seem redundant. To most people, bonsai appear to be miniature trees, and rightly so. The plantings so commonly seen are, after all, dwarfed versions of their full-size counterparts in nature. So what is a miniature bonsai? To answer that question precisely, let's examine the definition of *bonsai*.

Bonsai is a compound word made up of two Japanese characters, *bon* and *sai* and *Bon* can be variously translated as "tray, pot, container, or vessel." *Sai* means "planting, plant, planted, or plantings." Combined, *bonsai* becomes simply some kind of planting in a container without reference to size, species, age, or style.

Common usage of the word *bonsai* includes all the varied nuances, perceptions, and preconceived notions we have come to associate with this ancient and fascinating art form. Most bonsai enthusiasts come in contact with bonsai at neighborhood garden centers, local club shows, county fairs, exhibits, and perhaps even mail order catalogs and large grocery stores. What most people observe are plants about 10 inches high. Thirty-inch-high bonsai, by contrast, are therefore, erroneously regarded as too large, cumbersome, and not as cute as their smaller equivalents. Most people, when asked to describe a bonsai, will hold their hands about 10 inches apart when describing their version of what they have come to know. Even the plastic bonsai marketed through import stores are only 6 to 8 inches tall.

However, the art of bonsai gives us a wide range of sizes from which to select, from 1 inch to 100 inches in height. We do not evaluate the merit of paintings by their size nor do we reject sculpture because it is too big or too small. Nor should we judge bonsai in this manner. Successful bonsai convey a sense of scale, proportion, and artistic merit independent of actual size. Bonsai artists simply choose the dimensions of their canvas just as the painter does.

When I first started collecting wild flowers and seedlings from the schoolyard over forty years ago, miniature containers seemed the most appropriate size because they visually balanced the delicate leaves and flowers. Today, I still have a soft place in my heart for these most precious of plantings—the smallest of the small, miniature bonsai.

1

INTRODUCTION TO MINIATURE BONSAI

A BRIEF HISTORY

The art and horticulture of bonsai has fascinated people for centuries. The actual history of bonsai remains somewhat uncertain and imprecise, not because we cannot trace its development, but because its early evolution was gradual. In ancient Egypt, for example, we can observe excellently preserved carvings and paintings of potted plants, both indoor and outdoor varieties, that graced the courtyards of kings, queens, and their important advisors. These plants are easily identified from the artwork even after all these years. They are native citrus trees—oranges, lemons, limes, kumquat, and their close relatives. We see palm trees and nut trees as well as graceful ferns, ornamental grasses, and flowers.

1–1

The problem is this: if we define *bonsai* as an artistically shaped plant in a container, then we will have to consider all the major ancient cultures that enjoyed cultivating trees in pots. Among these cultures are ancient Greece, Rome, India, and the vast Mongolian empire, as well as early Europeans. But if we choose to define *bonsai* as an Oriental art, we would be forced to discount or diminish the contributions by previous civilizations. In China, by the year 200 A.D., established styles of dwarf trees were associated with all the major provinces. They had fun names like the "earthworm" style of Szechwan, the "dancing dragon" style of Anhwe and the "three winding" style of Northern China. Chinese techniques of training trees were so advanced at this time that skillful horticulturists could twist the trunks of their trees into the calligraphy of the Chinese alphabet. Some artists formed their trees into significant word phrases and expressions denoting "age," "beauty," "perseverance," and other important words. Other artists worked to sculpt living tree trunks into the images of the crane, tortoise, bear, or other meaningful animal shapes, mythological or symbolic.

1–2

Most bonsai literature credits the Japanese with originating bonsai. The words *bon* (**1–1**) and *sai* (**1–2**), pronounced "bone" and "sigh," are certainly Japanese, but their Chinese equivalents, *p'en* and *t'sai*, look identical in calligraphy. As Japan emerged from an isolated island into a world-class power, a tremendous influx of foreign people, products, and philosophy were responsible for the nation we see today. With regard to bonsai, the artistic skills that Buddhist monks brought to this developing nation were embraced by a people hungry for its meaningful attributes (**1–3**).

1–3

Let's consider the reclusive lifestyle of the early Japanese Buddhist monk (**1–4**). He has a small private room of his own adjacent to an open outdoor courtyard (**1–5**). On a simple wooden stand rests a windswept pine tree that he gathered from the nearby mountains. He tends his prized tree carefully, removing errant twigs while trying to maintain the natural look of a wild tree. He waters, fertilizers, and looks after his possession, doting over it with the watchful eye of a mother hen, much to the concern of his teachers and superiors. He enjoys gazing upon his tree for hours at a time because it brings him back to the grandeur of the Japanese Alps where he likes to hike whenever possible (**1–6**). His meditation time is meaningful and profound when he focuses on this miniature survivor.

A fictitious account? Perhaps not, for it is well documented that the earliest bonsai known in Japan were associated with the monasteries. When Europe had seen its first bonsai, around the turn of the century, the art form was naturally associated with Japan. Early American bonsai were either imported directly from Japan or produced in the backyards and courtyards of Japanese–Americans. Their impact on American bonsai is firmly entrenched in history. Their contributions to this historical art form cannot be overstated. Through these ethnic corridors, we now know much more about bonsai than we did only forty years ago. There are no secrets about keeping them alive. What's

1–4

1–5

1-6

required is simply an attentive, caring eye and good horticultural practice. Bonsai do require special soil, unique tools, and regular, consistent attention, but that's all.

As a nine-year-old schoolboy, I was oddly fascinated with the idea of transplanting small flowers and seedlings from the wild. I would place them ever so carefully into containers and nurture them on my bedroom windowsill. I'd plant wild columbine in the hollow of an interestingly shaped stone. I'd carefully transplant hemlock into the halves of walnut shells. One of my mother's thimbles housed a tiny crocus bulb. Ferns, decorative grasses, and ivy occupied containers fashioned from acorn husks, teacups, and whatever else I could find, build, or modify for my purposes. Discarded saucers were hoarded. Tin pans from small meat pies were carefully washed out and perforated for use as a seedling bed. Each day, I dutifully recorded careful measurements and observations in a notebook and stashed it away in a secret hiding place behind the wall paneling. If I discovered a new color of violet on my way home from school, I immediately dug it up, using any available sharp stick, or perhaps lunch

spoon, and tucked it away into a shirt pocket for safe-keeping. Sometimes this was not safe, due to my short memory at this age.

Years later when a friend gave me my first bonsai book, I felt as though I had finally received the validation I so craved. To imagine that others might be out there who were concerned with the miniaturization of flora was astounding. Learning that centuries of history were behind this established art form was nearly beyond my comprehension.

REQUIREMENTS FOR SUCCESS

Recently, a new bonsai club member came to my nursery to observe me at work on my bonsai (**1-7**). It was late July and I had already watered my plants well before greeting my guest. We wandered around benches, empty seedling trays, and the heeling-in area for growing in the ground. I described the things in process. Some trees were waiting in the ground to thicken their trunks, and others were just recovering from having the strong apex removed. A maple grove, recently defoliated, was just showing signs of swelling leaf buds. Some three-year-old crab apple trees were developing their first fruiting spurs for next year. I thought the tour had been quite successful and informative as we headed for the exit, until my visitor said, "But you didn't *do anything*!"

1-7

This beginner knew that I cared for thousands of plants and had the notion that I would be overworked, with trimmers trimming and tweezers tweezing, and she supposed she would get to view this mad spectacle. She hoped to quickly learn the shortcuts, trade secrets, and practical knowledge not found in books. She wanted to observe, take notes, and after a few hours, grasp bonsai-growing secrets.

We took another tour of the bonsai nursery. When we came to the first bonsai, an elm, I pointed out that the new growth was an even grass green color as compared to the earlier growth which showed dark green veins on light green leaves. "This shows me that my fertilizer application ten days ago was just right," I told her. We went to the next plant, a pine. "The size of this candle shows that my total candle removal on May 20th was a bit too severe. I should have retained some of the smaller ones." Moving to the defoliated maple grove, I said, "It's good to see these new leaf buds swell up like this. It means that, in about a week, I can water it like the others instead of withholding moisture due to decreased transpiration."

We talked about each tree and observed minute details, such as the temperature of the container, undersides of the foliage, and lichens on the trunks. Each was an indicator of the bonsai's health. Each bonsai had its own story to tell for the grower willing to observe closely enough. The plants themselves were the proof of success or failure for those willing to accept the results of their observations. This cause-and-effect relationship is measured in weeks, months, or seasons.

As we finished this second garden tour, my visitor recognized that we indeed had "done something"—we'd taken the time to observe results. The requirement for success is simple—enjoy the responsibility for caring for a whole plant in a container that depends on you for its every need. A teacher can observe scores of schoolchildren at play without incident, but unobserved children can get into serious trouble within minutes. Care and observation pay off, and neglect will quickly be recognized. If I have to take out the pruning tools and remove a bunch of foliage from one of my bonsai in August, I know my earlier efforts have failed.

Ideally, the successful bonsai grower has three important traits. First, the grower feels the need to nurture a living plant, obtaining satisfaction from the caring process and gratification from its growth and development. The grower is sad when responsible for killing a plant, but he does not give up and tries to do better next time. Second, the bonsai grower is willing and eager to experiment, observe, or take action. The grower is not afraid to prune, and, even more important, he's willing to observe the results of pruning. Failure to achieve new growth in the proper direction is not perceived as failure; it's merely information to use to prune differently next time. Third, the grower must be strong enough so that the results of his efforts constitute sufficient reward. Depending on the advice of others distracts from the personal joy bonsai can bring. When the grower's best trees were fashioned by others, even "experts," the grower misses an important aspect of creating original art.

MINIATURE BONSAI

My earliest experiences with bonsai were easy since I happened to select miniature bonsai to start with. The plants dug from the wild were 6 to 8 inches tall at most. Some were as small as 3 inches. I learned easily from these plants. I was attracted to them because they were free, cute, and easy to dig.

But there were other reasons. Had I dug up a larger plant, I would have had no pot to plant it in. It would have to be planted somewhere in the yard. Also, the space limitations on my bedroom windowsill made it prohibitive to secure anything wider than 3 inches, or the plant would tumble to the floor.

My qualifications—free, cute, and easy to dig—are still good criteria for choosing plants for miniature bonsai.

Free. I have taught beginning bonsai classes at a community college for twenty-five years. My courses were designed to familiarize students with the essentials of growing these miniature trees. Many students were on a tight budget, and they were attracted to a hobby that encourages stress reduction. It seemed inappropriate to require materials for this class. And I felt a responsibility to instruct them in using plant material at little or no cost.

Volunteer seedlings provide the easiest and most readily available material. All around town, you can find naturally occurring sprouts from fallen seed under mature trees. Sharp-eyed students found sources of seedlings and reported their location in the next class. Soon a deluge of free seedlings was passed around the class for the others to enjoy. Together we designed maple groves, elm forests, simple rock plantings, and, of course, the inevitable windswept juniper—all on a miniature scale. The work was enthusiastic, inspired, and satisfying. I even suspect that students who shelled out perfectly good money to local garden centers were a bit jealous!

Gathering plants from the wild can be just as rewarding and equally as inexpensive. The next time you travel, carry along digging implements, containers, and potting soil. You may be surprised where you might run across a cute little hemlock or wild cherry. Ask at your local ranger station when in doubt. Most permits, when offered, are free. Other restrictions apply for plants that are endangered, being resold, or larger than what you seek. Exchange seedlings and information with fellow bonsai enthusiasts. It's a great way to share your knowledge and make new friends.

Cute. Have you ever noticed, when the local bonsai club puts on a display, how much attention the miniatures get? The uneducated public responds most favorably to miniature bonsai. I have attended hundreds of bonsai shows as exhibitor, judge, babysitter, question-answerer, or just plain observer. It is astonishing to see a group of adults quickly glance at an eighty-year-old pine, then move to a miniature crab apple and begin to talk baby talk to each other. The attraction is unmistakable and the charm is universal.

Easy to dig. I would love to be able to find the perfect hundred-year-old pine tree in the woods. I would like it

to be naturally stunted; just a foot high with good trunk taper, well-placed branches, compact foliage, and roots no more than 10 inches long. Dream on. After all my collecting, I have gained huge respect for older specimens. Frankly, the trees with the greatest chance of transplanting success are the smaller and younger ones. I get no satisfaction digging out a venerable old tree after five hours' work only to watch it slowly die in my yard. Small to medium-size trees are ten times as likely to survive, and they can be trained into acceptable bonsai just by reducing their height. This gives you a well-proportioned miniature bonsai with some actual age on it that is rewarding and noticeable.

Advantages of Growing Miniature Bonsai

They're easy to grow.

At major bonsai conventions, guest lecturers and demonstrators usually do a "first styling" of a sizable plant specimen. After offering design philosophy, the lecturer makes a crude sketch of the proposed finished product and begins work on the tree, often with assistants. Three or four hours later, the finished bonsai more or less resembles the drawing, and the bonsai master carefully explains that the bonsai is not quite finished. They've run out of time but established the basic design. Whoever wins the tree will be responsible for the finishing touches.

Rarely do these conventions address miniature bonsai. When they do, it is usually just as a supplemental lecture or small group seminar. Miniature bonsai are simply finished too quickly and a main event of miniatures would need to style several.

The beginner can easily see the advantage. If it takes three professional bonsai masters four hours to partially complete the styling of a large bonsai, how long would it take a beginning student? So, miniature bonsai has distinct advantages in size alone. It's easy to carry to class, more manageable to move around during styling, and it requires a smaller pot with, of course, less bonsai soil. But perhaps the greatest advantage is that the project can be completed in just an hour or two. This time frame appeals to most first-time bonsai students. If there is dead wood to carve, it is manageable in size and does not require power tools. Pruning can be finished in a matter of minutes, potting is easy, and there's less mess to clean up. It is possible to style a miniature bonsai right on the kitchen table in thirty minutes, including cleanup time. This size of bonsai is just plain fun to do. It's simple, quick, requires little space, and it's not as serious. In just a few minutes, beginners can turn out something to be proud of. They can show it to others and make them smile. This makes miniature bonsai the best choice for the novice.

Drawbacks to Growing Miniature Bonsai

Growing miniature bonsai is special and, so, requires special care. The plants' diminutive size makes ordinary care impossible.

They dry out more quickly than larger bonsai. The small container contains a tiny root ball that simply cannot store as much reserve water as its larger counterparts. A bonsai that's half the size of another actually has one-eighth the soil volume. A container of soil 2 inches on each side has a volume of 8 cubic inches. A bonsai container 4 inches on each side has a whopping 64 cubic inches of soil volume—eight times greater! In rough terms, it is not unreasonable to assume that if the 4-inch pot were to completely dry out every twenty-four hours, the 2-inch pot would dry out in only three hours.

Obviously, miniature bonsai require special care in summer when you'll need to make major adjustments in the watering schedule. For people who work long hours away from home, the responsibility of raising these tiny plants may be too much. Consider larger containers and plants that tolerate dryness, such as pine or juniper, if you don't have time for watering.

Smaller containers also freeze more quickly. So, winter care is critical. Bonsai in large containers can survive sudden drops in temperature. Their volume alone allows them to survive overnight frost or cold, drying winds. Locate miniature bonsai in a protective surrounding, such as a cold frame, well in advance of the first freeze to guarantee their survival. Just one sudden unseasonable cold snap can wreak havoc with a collection of tiny bonsai. Plan ahead and anticipate these events to ensure your success in growing miniatures.

When insects and disease attack smaller plants, damage is more obvious than such an attack on larger specimens. If a tiny elm tree only has twenty leaves, a caterpillar can do tremendous damage overnight. The same caterpillar on a large street tree might go unnoticed for weeks before the damage calls attention to the problem, and, even then, it does not threaten the tree's life. A miniature bonsai with all its leaves dam-

aged by insects late in August won't have enough growing season left that summer and fall to grow a new batch of leaves. It may die. That's why you'll need to watch over your miniature trees. Early treatment is essential when problems occur, but even better is an extensive preventive pest-control program. Well designed benches, routine spraying of surrounding surfaces, garden litter pickup, and regular inspection of the area around the trees are ways to prevent problems before they happen.

It's important to pay attention to the needs of your bonsai with several visits to the plant during the day. You need to closely and thoroughly observe *each* plant, making sure that you neglect no aspect of the bonsai. When caring for miniature bonsai, these requirements are even greater than for larger trees. If you have a table full of miniature bonsai, it's easy to make the mistake of watering all of them simultaneously instead of watering each one as its individual moisture demands dictate. Similarly, if you've made up a batch of fungicide for your miniature quince, it's tempting to spray all your miniatures whether they need it or not. This is poor bonsai management, regardless of size, but the temptation to care for miniature bonsai this way is even stronger. Get into the habit of paying close attention to the individual, unique needs of each plant, and resist the urge to lump bonsai together merely on the basis of size. It is always more appropriate to treat a miniature juniper more like a juniper than like a miniature. The term *miniature* is only a size classification, not a guide to its care. For a complete and more specific guide to the care and maintenance of miniature bonsai, see chapter 8.

BONSAI SIZE CLASSIFICATIONS

When I first started out in bonsai, I was fascinated with miniature flowers, fruits, and berries. As I increased my number of plants, I found diversified species and varied sizes. At first, nothing pleased me more than the tiny annuals, perennials, and bulbs. Soon, the windswept juniper and twisted pine drew my attention as well, and I enjoyed deciduous tree forms, too. Because of this diversity, I soon recognized the need to maintain an appropriate scale for each tree. While it was easy to keep a bonsai rosemary quite small, it was useless to try to form a good-looking white oak under 10 inches tall.

The size of the tree became a concession to the reality that some trees, and some styles of trees, had to be increased in size. I resisted the tendency to get larger plants because I felt that the whole point of bonsai was to achieve the look of a full-size tree in as small a scale as was physically and biologically possible.

I now know that that self-imposed rule kept me from enjoying an even larger array of species, styles, and methods. When I saw my first bonsai masterpieces in Japan, I was astonished and a little dismayed. I had been trying to achieve an impossible grandeur and detail in bonsai under 15 inches tall. Before me stood bonsai 30, 40, and even 50 inches high. I felt somewhat betrayed. No wonder calendar pictures contained so much detail. It's easy to get fifteen branches all perfectly arranged around a 3-foot-high trunk, so where's the challenge? Of course, this was before I'd seen bonsai with heights of 80, 90, and 100 inches.

In time, of course, we all reach our own personal comfort levels. I adjusted to the idea that beauty is unrelated to size. Just because one bonsai artist chooses to work in miniature does not invalidate the work of others who prefer the stately presence only a large tree can bring. Indeed, the notion that a tree can determine its own ideal size is a valid and noble artistic concept. Japanese homes display bonsai as the room itself dictates. A large room usually has a large bonsai. Miniature bonsai are only displayed in smaller, more intimate spaces. I couldn't help but think back to the size of my childhood bedroom and its 4-inch windowsill. I might have preferred larger bonsai right from the start had I been raised in a larger environment.

Today, we're familiar with many sizes of bonsai. Their exact sizes and corresponding names are sometimes confusing and inexact. Translations vary and further difficulties arise when converting Japanese and metric measurements to inches and feet. Also, the largest bonsai *shapes* we know are not bonsai at all. Remember that the *bon* in *bonsai* means "pot." A larger Japanese-style tree in the ground may resemble a bonsai in style, shape, and character, but technically it isn't a bonsai at all. It's called a *niwa-gi*, regardless of size.

The largest common size, called *imperial bonsai*, measures from 60 inches to around a maximum of 120 inches high. They are considered an eight-handed size, implying that the services of four or more people is required to move one about. The name comes from the appearance of fine, stately old bonsai around the interior of the Imperial Palace, residence of Japan's emperor.

Large bonsai—less than 60 inches tall but more than 40 inches—are classified as *hachi-uye*. These big garden bonsai are sometimes temporarily displayed in halls, courtyards, and entryways large enough to handle their imposing visual impact. They are considered four- to eight-handed bonsai in terms of their weight.

Most large bonsai are considered *dai* bonsai, or *omono* bonsai. They range between 30 and 48 inches in height. Two or three people can carry one, and they're displayed in rooms larger than 16 by 18 feet, or 288 square feet.

Two-handed bonsai is the size most commonly seen in bonsai shows. They range from 16 to 36 inches high and are called *chiu* bonsai, or *chumono* bonsai. They require only an average-size room for best display, say a large entrance hall, a modest living room, or a large bedroom.

Medium-size bonsai are known as *katade-mochi* bonsai, sometimes spelled as *kotate* or *kotade*. These trees can be carried in one hand. They are the most popular size and account for the greatest number of bonsai of any classification. They are between 10 and 18 inches high.

The small, or *komono*, bonsai can be easily picked up and carried by one hand. It is between 6 and 10 inches in height. It fits easily in the hand and constitutes the largest of the miniature bonsai (**1–8**).

1–8

Mame bonsai are known as pocket bonsai, or palm bonsai, because several can fit in the palm of a hand. They are usually less than 6 inches high but more than 2 inches high. The size classification *shohin* bonsai is somewhat smaller (**1–9**).

Shito bonsai, or *keshitsubo* bonsai, are the smallest of all. Their maximum size is around 2 inches high and includes anything smaller that's horticulturally possible. English translations include the names "poppy seed bonsai," "fingertip bonsai," and "pea-size bonsai." These plants, pot and all, will fit on a fingertip and certainly test the growing skills of the enthusiast.

1–9

As you can see from the chart Bonsai Classifications, these size classifications are overlapping and a bit imprecise; however, this does not detract from what they indicate. Their very existence gives the bonsai artist a full range of canvases on which to create art. The advantages of miniature sizes far outweigh the disadvantages. They are highly portable, easily obtained, easy to make, and provide more satisfaction in a shorter period of time than their larger counterparts. If you ever thought you might be interested in starting this fascinating hobby, miniatures could be the answer. They give you an affordable, accessible, no-frills beginning. Their gratification is instant, their biology nonthreatening, and their art simple and satisfying.

Bonsai Classifications

Large Bonsai

Imperial bonsai	eight-handed bonsai	60 to 80 inches
Hachi-uye bonsai	six-handed bonsai	40 to 60 inches
Dai bonsai	four-handed bonsai	30 to 48 inches
Omono bonsai	four-handed bonsai	30 to 48 inches

Medium Bonsai

Chiu bonsai	two-handed bonsai	16 to 36 inches
Chumono bonsai	two-handed bonsai	16 to 36 inches
Katade-mochi bonsai	one-handed bonsai	10 to 18 inches

Miniature Bonsai

Komono bonsai	one-handed bonsai	6 to 10 inches
Mame bonsai	one-handed bonsai	5 to 8 inches
Shohin bonsai	palm-size bonsai	2 to 6 inches
Shito bonsai	fingertip bonsai	2 to 4 inches
Keshitsubo bonsai	poppy seed-size bonsai	1 to 3 inches

2

THE DWARFING
PROCESS

Understanding underlying forces that make bonsai small is important for growers trying to achieve scale and clarity of design within the framework of healthy horticultural practice. For bonsai of average size, these principles are important to achieve success. In growing miniature bonsai, they're especially important because you're attempting to grow the smallest of the small. Where dwarfing principles normally interest bonsai growers, in miniature bonsai they become the foundation of success, the knowledge behind the illusion, the process that forms the art.

Consider these forces carefully, because they can help you achieve your objectives. Ignore them and your task will be great. The finest miniature bonsai often display the successful combination of two or more of these factors. Rarely can you rely on just one force to compact the plant sufficiently. In combination, they're very powerful indeed. Leaf reductions even to 1 percent of normal size are possible! Imagine reducing a foot-long leaf down to ⅛ inch! It can be done. With difficulty, of course, but it's still possible.

The three main sources of dwarfing are *genetics*, *natural forces*, and *horticultural manipulation*. Let's consider these carefully, each in turn.

GENETIC DWARFS

Just as the name implies, a *genetic dwarf* is small due to its genetic code. Plant husbandry is thousands of years old, and gardeners have long collected rare, unusual, or strikingly beautiful plants. Natural variation in the plant population is responsible for the majority of species we see today. In the last few hundred years, however, we have been increasingly able to manipulate the genetic code. This has been accomplished, not at the cellular level, but through the process of selection in much the same way that nature does. One wheat field survives an unusually early frost while another field nearby is damaged. The following year, both fields are planted with wheat from the cold-resistant field. Agriculturists, horticulturists, botanists, and geneticists attempt to improve our food crops to make them resistant to disease, larger in size, better in flavor, and easier to harvest.

But what about bonsai? Is it possible to genetically engineer a plant to form itself into an artistically shaped plant solely on the basis of its genetic code? The nursery trade has made giant steps toward such a real-ity, but we're not there yet! What we have is a vast array of available plant material that would not exist without taking advantage of coaxed natural selection. I collect seeds from all over the world. Each year I sow seeds that I feel will be appropriate for bonsai. Some seeds sprout, some do not. A portion of the seedlings develops fungus; others do not. Some first-year plants look promising; still others are simply unsuitable for one reason or another. I can collect seed from the promising plants and see if its superior traits can be passed on to the next generation.

What I am doing is not so different from what the early geneticist Gregor Mendel did in the garden of his monastery. I am manipulating the genetics of plants based on their physical appearance, selecting individuals with superior bonsai traits, and propagating them again into the next generation to see if particular alterations become part of the genetic code. This same process has produced thousands of wonderful new varieties of plants suitable for bonsai purposes unavailable in the wild. If we were to depend solely on nature for our bonsai material, we would be dependent on the stressed high-altitude plants from the timberline, tundra, and desert. Natural selection has made these plants truly hardy, but unfortunately in the relatively sheltered confines of the bonsai pot they revert to a more sheltered form.

Consider these two crab apple seedlings (**2–1**). Both came from the same tree, yet one obviously has red leaves and the other, green. This is a good example of genetic variation from seed. The green crab apple will always be green. Every leaf will come out that color month after month in the growing season. Even the

2–1

brand new leaves will come out green. I also have some apples whose leaves are all green, but the newly emerging leaves are always red, like photinia. If I were to graft the red crab apple on top of the green crab apple, the upper leaves would be red and the lower leaves below the graft would remain green. If I were to grow these branches from cuttings, the resulting tree would always be the same color as the parent branch.

Next, let's compare these two crab apples (2–2). The tree on the left is quite normal in every way. The tree on the right is very similar in every aspect but one: its leaves are naturally cut into three distinct lobes similar to the trident maple. This unusual mutation makes the crab apple on the right superior bonsai material. Its leaves will be more interesting. As you can see, natural genetic mutations can affect leaf color, leaf shape, and most importantly, leaf size, as shown in the next example.

2–2

These two crab apples (2–3) are the same age, have been cared for identically, and are in the same size container. Simple genetics accounts for the large differences between them. The plant on the left grows slowly, has large leaves, and is prone to powdery mildew. Its trunk is naturally straight and it does not retain its lower leaves well. The plant on the right grows with vigor, has small leaves, is resistant to disease, its trunk is naturally curved (I did not twist this trunk), and it buds back readily while retaining its lower branches. Obviously, if we were to choose one of these plants as miniature bonsai material, the crab apple on the right would be vastly superior.

2–3

Some genetic mutations are saved for bonsai purposes and propagated by grafting or by cuttings just for that purpose. If I were to propagate the superior crab apple for miniature bonsai, I could perhaps market it with my own chosen name, even patent it! This same principle goes on year after year among experimental nursery propagators. In the large Chinese elm family, there are dozens of known genetic mutations. For miniature bonsai, the *seiju* elm and the *hokkaido* elm are obvious choices.

Most plant species now have dwarf varieties, due to the efforts of plant propagators and research botanists. We now enjoy a vast array of plant material that did not exist just a hundred years ago. Enjoy these wonderful genetic dwarfs. They're perfect for miniature bonsai use. Employing additional bonsai horticultural practice, you can make a genetic dwarf even smaller.

Let's consider some things besides genetics that help to dwarf plants. Those that occur in nature without human intervention are called natural forces. Following each natural force, I present the bonsai culture equivalent. Since neither of these forces involves the genetics of the plant, once the force is removed, the plant will automatically revert to its unstressed form.

NATURAL FORCES AND THEIR BONSAI CULTURE EQUIVALENTS

Wind

It is common knowledge that a plant growing in a windy area is shaped differently than a similar plant growing in a calm setting (2–4). Compare the cypress that grows next to the ocean with those located farther inland. Wind is indeed a powerful shaping force. Plants stressed by wind are more compact. They grow close to the ground, have short internodes and smaller leaves, and their branches are tightly clumped together in "clouds" of foliage. I hardly recommend growing your bonsai in front of an electric fan. However, you can do some things to take advantage of this natural force.

Place your bonsai on an elevated bench. This makes them look more attractive and accessible, and it also allows an increased passage of breeze around and through the bonsai. This increased circulation will decrease leaf size and help the plant fight off disease as well. Mildew and fungus will not thrive in a well-ventilated area. Resist the natural tendency to shelter your bonsai near a fence, wall, or large tree. The air is relatively still near these obstacles. Get your bonsai out into the open where the air is constantly in motion. If your trees need more shade, cover them with an overhead canopy of lattice work or shade cloth.

2–4

Rain

When you compare the leaves of tropical plants and desert plants, you can easily see how moisture levels affect their size (**2–5**). Some equatorial plants have enormous leaves 6, 8, even 10 feet long. In the harsh desert, plants have evolved a way to drop their tiny leaves completely during extra-dry spells.

Bonsai respond similarly. Both underwatering and overwatering can be fatal to a plant, but within the healthy range in between, you can control leaf size with water alone. A heavily watered plant or a plant that's kept just a bit too much on the wet side is a pampered large-leaved plant. If you water only when the plant needs it, you can dwarf the leaf size a bit. New buds will be closer together, leaf stems will not extend as far, and the leaf area will be reduced as the plant tries to conserve moisture. I grow zelkova elm from cuttings taken from a large tree in my yard. The rooted cuttings are grown in the ground for a few years to help develop some trunk size. Recently I compared two branches. One branch was taken from a plant about 20 feet from the house. It had nice small leaves, delicate branchlets, and short internodes. The other branch was taken from under my roof downspout. Zelkova is very tolerant of overwatering and the second branch grew into a healthy, vigorous specimen, with large leaves, a lack of secondary branches, long leaf stems, and wide internodes. I could not attribute these differences to genetics since the two branches were cuttings from the same parent plant. They both received the same amount of sun, are the same age, and neither was restricted by a pot. Perhaps there was a nutrition difference? I doubt that there is much nutrition in water coming off my asphalt roof. Water alone must have accounted for their size difference.

Fertilizer

In nature plants get small, sustained doses of nutrients—some from minerals in the soil, some from the atmosphere, and some from decomposing organic matter (**2–6**). Even microorganisms in the soil help the plant process these nutrients. In a container at home, a bonsai is forced to rely on its grower to provide this function. Soil nutrients are soon depleted and must be supplemented. In a bonsai pot microorganisms are minimal. Decaying organic matter cannot be shared with surrounding trees and animals. It is well established that fertilizer helps grow nice, big green leaves, but more appropriate to the bonsai grower is the knowledge that modest amounts of nutrients can make *small* leaves.

Soil

It is hard to isolate the influence of soil on plants separate from the closely related influences of nutrition and moisture (**2–7**). In the mountains, a lone pine

2–5

THE DWARFING PROCESS

23

2–6

2–7

tree grows in a soil primarily made of rock that has been decomposed by freezing and thawing over a long period of time. Certainly this extremely course soil is also well drained and has little nutrition as well. A little-known fact, however, is that the shape of the soil particles can affect the shape of the plant. Japanese growers have taken advantage of this phenomenon. If you place a pine seedling in jagged rocky soil, its roots will divide and redivide at a greater rate than they would in polished sandy soil. To me, this makes sense; however, the next part is a little hard to believe unless you try it yourself. The pine with jagged roots will produce jagged branches. There's some natural force at work here, and the grower can take advantage of it to help influence the growth and development of bonsai. The effect is subtle, to be sure, but still usable as yet another way to grow better bonsai.

The Container

When an embattled dwarf pine (2–8) is observed near timberline, it is often growing in a rock crevice. Several hundred years ago, a pine nut got caught in that crevice where it found shelter, nutrition, and moisture. Gradually and persistently, the seedling's roots spread out in all directions searching for oxygen, water, and more nutrients. After a few years, the medium-size pine tree started growing more stunted and dwarfed because the roots had exhausted the container. New roots replaced old roots at a slow rate. Moisture was precious and nutrition was very sparse. Our bonsai containers duplicate this scenario. We can dwarf leaves quite easily by using the pot alone.

The odd part about this otherwise obvious natural phenomenon is that the difference in size is almost immediate. If you place five identical cuttings in con-

2–8

tainers ranging from 1 to 5 gallons in size, the growth differences are noticeable after only a few months. The roots still have not even reached the sides of the container. I suspect this growth gradient is due to the increased temperature and moisture stability found in large containers. In any case, it is a real, useful tool to help you grow plants large or small, as you choose.

Snow

Did you ever wonder why deciduous trees have branches that angle up while conifers have branches that slope down? Often it's due to winter snow load. The leafless twigs of deciduous trees cannot accumulate snow to the extent that winter evergreen conifers can. The characteristic downward angle of high-altitude conifers is often duplicated by training bonsai branches down with copper wire. The visual effect is

striking and immediately seems to age the tree.

The pine tree in **2–9** was shaped entirely by snow. It has never been wired. Notice the extreme downward slant of all the branches. This tree could have easily been shaped in this fashion by using copper wire; however, the principle is the same. When spring comes in the mountains, the new growth points upwards, but when the fall snow arrives, the hardened-off new growth is forced back down. Here's a good wiring lesson straight from nature.

2–9

Bud Selection

When deer browse around in spring looking for food, what do you suppose they look for on a pine tree? Last year's tough needles? Small buds growing inside along the sides of the branches? Of course not. They munch off the tenderest and longest candles that protrude from the branch ends. This is basically how we keep our bonsai small as well. By pruning off succulent new growth each spring, we not only limit the outer dimensions of the plant, but we encourage secondary growth.

The two Scotch pines in **2–10** are genetically the same, and they're the same age. The larger plant on the right had its largest candles removed in the late spring,

2-10

until later. On deciduous trees, the outer large buds are easy to see. Not only can you prevent unwanted long buds from sprouting, but you can also stimulate the formation of more inner buds at the same time. By the time the true spring arrives a month later, the remaining buds will be more compact, numerous, and smaller. Smaller buds means dwarf leaves in the spring.

2-11

its only pruning this year. The small pine on the left had the following pruning regimen: On May 15 this year, all the candles were removed, regardless of size. On June 15, all the largest of the candles that had regrown were removed entirely. On August 15, all the largest candles that had regrown again were pinched in half, and all of last year's needles were pulled off. This photo was taken at the end of September.

You can easily see the size difference in the needles. None of the needles were cut in half; these are full-size needles without the brown tips from trimming with pruning shears. Notice that next year's buds are also smaller. This coming spring, the candles will be shorter. Constant pruning dwarfs the next generation of growth. This is yet another dwarfing force that you can use to create excellent miniature bonsai.

What we have just accomplished by pruning is something that duplicates nature. Plants in stressed environments are constantly pruned by foraging animals, frostbite, insects, disease, wind damage, extreme desiccation, and snow load. We can simulate these natural forces with our own imposed cultural forces.

Frostbite

Frostbite (2–11) can happen either in early spring or late fall. It usually doesn't happen in the dead of winter because trees are prepared for the cold. They are quite dormant. Spring frostbite happens when warm, early spring precedes a sudden cold snap. The tree has just started to grow and this tender young growth, not yet fully developed, is killed by the cold. The inner buds and the smaller, tighter buds are often left undamaged.

Extreme early spring pruning of branch tips on bonsai has a distinct advantage as compared to waiting

Late fall frostbite catches the semidormant tree at a time when next year's buds have just formed and still contain water and sap. These buds are killed as well as the tender, thin stems that supply their nutrients. The results of this damage are not seen until spring, but the damage has already happened. The tree, not having enough energy and physiological activity to heal itself in late fall, merely cordons off the living areas of the tree from the damaged twigs and buds. The following spring, the tree ignores its dead areas and concentrates on setting new terminal and lateral buds near the outermost still-living branchlets. The dead twigs turn black and fall off, presenting the viewer with the classic visual case of dieback.

The bonsai grower can decide in late fall which of the outermost twigs to remove instead of allowing nature to decide. Pretend your pruning shears are Jack Frost himself. Where would he attack? No doubt the most susceptible growth would be the long, succulent shoots that started to form just after the heat of summer was over. This fall growth is long and leggy due to the decreased length of the day, lower angle of the sun, increased moisture of fall rains, and increased root activity of the tree in general. Trim off this growth now. It is usually too large and located in the wrong place anyway. Shorten all branches a bit at this time and the new spring buds will be smaller, particularly at the branch terminals. In the spring, the leaves will be smaller.

Insects

If you think insects have no effect on leaf size, look again. They attack the largest and most succulent leaves and buds first. This long, new maple branch (**2–12**) is a good example. Their sucking action slows sap and drains the whole system slightly. New buds formed during an insect attack do not form larger to compensate for sap depletion; they're formed smaller. These newly formed secondary smaller buds, if undamaged by insects, will open up to reveal very nice small leaves.

I certainly do not recommend the intentional application of sucking insects or borers to your bonsai for the purpose of dwarfing leaves (although medicine still uses leeches). Better yet, study these areas of attack where insects might tend to congregate. Remove terminal tips that are too large (as in the photo). Remove congested areas or shaded branches where the sun doesn't shine. Remember, your eyes are the sun and your pruning tool is an insect mandible looking for hidden juicy tidbits of foliage. Remove these susceptible areas, and your bonsai will be light, airy, and resistant to pests and disease. Your new growth will remain tough and compact at all times.

Disease

Where insects tend to attack the strongest shoots, disease tends to take advantage of the weak. If a branch does not receive enough light, it steadily weakens,

2–12

which encourages branches directly opposite on the other side of the trunk. At the same time, the branch directly below the weak branch grows progressively stronger as more and more light is able to reach it. The pattern of strength versus decay is responsible for the gradual removal of opposite branches and whorled branches typically found on young pine trees. Did you ever notice that old pine trees no longer exhibit this pattern of branches arranged like spokes on a wheel around the trunk?

Your pruning tool can encourage or discourage growth. Often the easiest way to encourage growth is to remove the competition to that growth. It is like thinking in reverse. Instead of pinching back new growth like an insect, remove the weaker branches around the area to encourage back budding, like disease eventually will if you don't. Your branches will be layered properly for the sun without distracting inner weak twigs and sickly branches. The overall health of your plant will be improved. It takes about three years for a dead pine branch to rot off. Why not just prune that weak branch off right now and get it over with? Don't

2–13

invite disease. Trim off those unsightly branches when they show signs of weakness. The remaining branches will get more sun, bud back nicely, and your bonsai will have a compact, alternating branch pattern that mimics older specimen trees in nature.

Wind Damage

We all admire the windswept trees at the beach, the angular conifers clinging to rocky gorges, or the embattled sentinels near timberline. These beautiful trees didn't get that way by having an easy life. Look closely at the trunk line and you will notice the number of times that these trees have put out unsuccessful branches or tops. Look closely at the photo (**2–13**). The shape of the trees is an indication of average wind velocity. I would guess that wind on this inland lake averages less than 5 miles per hour. Contrast this with **2–4** or **2–11**. If a tree has five successful branches, it might have had a dozen more if it were not for the harsh conditions under which it grows. Wind certainly

is a powerful force in these extreme environments.

We can choose to style a windswept tree by bending branches away from the "wind" using copper wire. We can physically break branches with our hands that grow against our imaginary wind. With pliers, carving tools, and lime sulfur, we can create in an hour a driftwood sculpture that would take the wind centuries to produce.

This western silver fir (**2–14**) looked quite like an ordinary shrub just a year ago. Using bonsai culture techniques designed to mimic nature, we can create the image of an old tree struggling to survive on a rocky ledge high above a windy valley. The apex is trimmed short to indicate a strong wind. The larger dead branch to the left suggests that an earlier trunk attempt was unsuccessful since it protruded too far from the protection of the ledge. The long, cascading branch twists and turns its way down the side of the mountain, seeking out relatively still air. To the right of the apex is a reminder of the wind's force—a sandblasted series of unsuccessful top shoots. In windy areas, growth usually

2–14

is stronger on the lower branches than on the exposed higher limbs. On the branch itself, these new buds will usually be located on either the lower side of the foliage or tucked well into the existing foliage "cloud."

By trimming off exposed buds on your bonsai, you accomplish the same task. New buds growing on the undersides of branches will not produce downward growth. This growth will always turn back upward and give a very nice appearance to the branch outline. Trim the top of the tree a bit more heavily than the bottom, just as the desert would. The upper areas of the tree carry more bud-inhibiting hormone than the lower areas. By removing more buds up high, you are actually removing this inhibiting hormone along with the buds, thereby stimulating new, smaller buds to form. In this manner, not only will new growth be more dwarfed, it will be more evenly distributed around the tree as well.

Snow Load

When you look at the intersection of a branch with its trunk on a tree that's accustomed to great snow, you notice several things. The angle of the branch is about 15 degrees below the horizontal plane. The branch is quite thick right at its junction with the trunk, and the downward curve is quite abrupt. That is, the branch is not bent down like a fishing rod. It's bent down at its extreme right at the trunk, and the branch gradually

rises up to 15 degrees below horizontal. How did that happen? The branch was bent when it was small.

The bonsai lesson here is this—select bonsai branches small enough to bend at this angle. If you attempt to save a larger branch, this branch must be broken down to avoid a fishing pole appearance. Some species are quite brittle; so, break your branches with care. I like to practice with prunings from the tree before intentionally cracking a branch still attached to the tree. You will find that if you wire the branch first, then you can let the partially damaged branch remain attached so it will naturally heal itself. For very large branches, I find it helpful to cut out a notch on the underside of the bend in order to make a steeper angle downward.

Summary

Nature creates interesting natural dwarfed trees in many ways, using powerful forces. These forces can be mimicked in our bonsai gardens utilizing certain accepted bonsai culture techniques. Even though our hands-on methods seem artificial at times, our art and horticulture derive inspiration directly from nature. Fine bonsai reflect this important relationship with our environment. Our methods may at times seem crude and irreverent, but we still cling to nature as our teacher. Let's not forget that precious relationship.

3

TOOLS & EQUIPMENT

PRUNING TOOLS

Part of what makes a hobby enjoyable is the tools and equipment. I encourage students to assemble an array of basic tools before attempting their first workshop project. Obviously, all these tools are not required. Some included here merely describe their importance and can introduce you to the wide variety of common household implements you can use to grow miniature bonsai. Look around your home for these tools. Ordinary sewing thread is useful for training miniature bonsai, but it's not sold in bonsai nurseries. Many other things around the house can help you get started without great cost. I've always enjoyed the creative and imaginative spirit of a student on a budget. A $20 root hook can be easily replaced by a bent tent stake or discarded salad fork. A wound sealer can be made out of shoe polish and carpenter's glue.

These tool suggestions are meant to inspire rather than discourage you. Engage your own resourcefulness. Use your imagination to gather the tools and equipment necessary to accomplish the creative task at hand.

The black tool at the bottom of **3–1** is perhaps the most common bonsai tool, a concave cutter. This tool is recommended for people starting out. The tool in the photo is forty years old, and its basic design has not changed for the last hundred years. The concave cutter allows you to cut off a branch close to the trunk. The cut, or scar remaining, is somewhat curved or concave, hence the name. For removing branches from the average size of bonsai, this is the most popular cutter. Just above the concave cutter is a larger form of the same tool. The larger tool is useful when working with hardwoods or collected plant stock from the mountains. That's because the longer handles give you more leverage for otherwise difficult cuts. The longer handles and cutting jaws make quick work of these tough woods. The next tool just above is a stainless steel copy of the common concave cutter. These silver-colored tools, introduced recently, have the advantage of being rust-free. They are a little harder to sharpen, but once sharpened, they hold their edge for years. With regular and timely maintenance, the black steel tools perform well enough. At the top of **3–1** is an unusual variety of concave cutters recommended for working on miniature bonsai. Their design allows them to remove small branches in tight places on normal-size bonsai. They function very well, however, as minibonsai concave cutters. The long handles and small cutting surface make

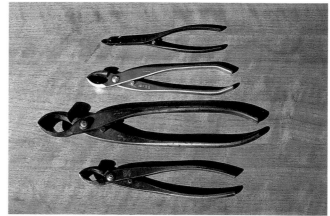

3–1

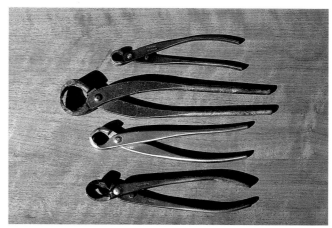

3–2

them a powerful tool indeed. They have the leverage necessary to make quick work of all *shohin* or smaller bonsai.

At the top of photo **3–2** is my favorite tool, small spherical knob cutters. The common concave cutters are curved in one direction. These spherical knob cutters produce a bowl-shaped scar that's concave in all directions, not just one. The cutting edges are designed to allow plenty of room for cut wood; therefore, this tool is superior in its ability to chew away at the trunk until you achieve the ideal contour. Other tools tend to skid off the mark and require tremendous hand pressure to make continuous alterations to a previously cut area. If I had to choose just one tool to do my work, this would be it. In **3–2**, second from the top is a large tool designed to cut roots. I find it particularly useful in removing tough taproots found on garden-grown bonsai stock or collected material from the woods. This tool is especially efficient for cutting due to its long handles and the large, clear area behind the cutting blades to accommodate freshly cut wood fragments. The stainless steel tool just below this is a large version of the spherical knob cutters. They hardly ever need sharpening and will last a lifetime. Smaller bonsai are more difficult to cut, but for cutting branches from ½ to 3 inches in diameter, this tool cannot be excelled. The bottom tool is unusual and hard to find. It's called angled spherical knob cutters. On this tool, the cutting blades of the more common spherical knob cutters have been slightly offset so that the advantages of the concave cutters and the spherical knob cutters can be combined. The design makes sense. In actual use, however, I can duplicate its performance with a combination of other tools.

The family of tools in **3–3** functions as simple scissors to cut small branches, twigs, and leaves. Any sharp shears or pointed pruning tool can serve this function as well. At the bottom is perhaps the best-selling bonsai tool of all time. This design, with its curving handles that enclose the fingers, has not changed for the last hundred years. It's in common use for light gardening, floral arranging, bonsai, and indoor crafts. Tools with a similar design are equally suitable. For more detailed and less repetitive tasks, the tool second from the bottom performs as well. The smaller finger loops accommodate only two fingers and fit smaller hands well. The sharp-pointed cutting blades are easy to aim toward obscure and detailed pruning work. The scissors just

above are a stainless-steel copy of the more popular bonsai trimming shears at the bottom. Again, the stainless cutting surfaces are tougher to sharpen, but they require less annual maintenance. The top tool is one I highly recommend for working with miniature bonsai. The finger loops are small and accommodate only one finger on one side and the thumb on the other. The cutting edges are specially beveled, so that they're tough enough to handle branches smaller than the diameter of a chopstick. I have also cut smaller gauges of copper wire (between 28 and 24 gauge) without damaging the tool.

Consider a collection of leaf trimmers in **3–4**, designed for repetitive cutting tasks that would be cum-

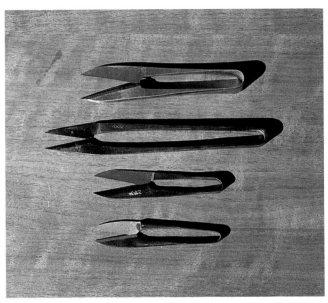

3–4

bersome for larger pruning tools. Simply use fingertips. Typically, they're used to remove larger leaves on deciduous bonsai in order to stimulate the production of smaller leaves. On conifers, these tools can shorten pine needles, thin out developing buds, or cut away strong vertical growth. The cutter on the bottom of the photograph is perhaps the least expensive tool offered at most bonsai nurseries. At around $3 it's a bargain. Above is a $10 version of the same design. Made of better-quality steel, this tool will last longer and it's easier to sharpen. Second from the top is a long-handled design that's great for bonsai growers who like maples, elm, birch, and other fast-growing species. The hand does not tire as easily during routine defoliation because pressure on the hand is more evenly distrib-

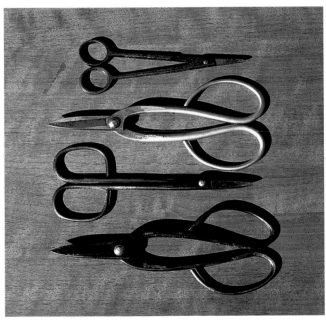

3–3

uted. At the top is a superior tool that's not only stainless-steel but has a curved working surface as well. The blades naturally fit the hand and enhance vision in congested areas. This is my favorite leaf trimmer. My wife uses a trimmer similar to this in her sewing projects—a simple Swedish tool made for cutting thread. I have secretly tried her trimmer on my bonsai with no apparent damage.

In the photo **3–5**, at the bottom is a traditional Japanese root hook. I have used this tool for twenty years. It has served me well and I'll probably never need to replace it. This tool loosens compacted soil, straightens out congested roots, and realigns circular roots into a more radial pattern around the bonsai trunk. Its wide wooden handle is easy to grip and pull. The pointed and curved metal working end is neither so sharp as to damage roots nor so dull as to be difficult to penetrate a root mass. The stainless-steel root fork above it is a commonly marketed root tool in bonsai nurseries. Its three tines loosen soil and straighten out roots on medium to small trees. The opposite end doubles as a potting spatula. The sharpened edges of this spatula cut around the periphery of a root ball contained in a pot. This helps to loosen the tree from the grip of a tight container. In addition, the flat, angled surface of the spatula serves to compact the soil surface after repotting. The tool's decorative handle doubles as a nonslip textured surface in the hand. More commonly seen as a root hook is a tool similar to the example with the red handle. This is a relatively inexpensive substitute for the tool with the wood handle shown at the bottom. The bent metal rod is sharpened at one end to

comb through roots, and the loop held in the hand is coated with rubberized material to make it easier to grip. The tool with the wood handle shown near the top is similar to the standard root hook shown at the bottom. Actually, this specialized tool is called a potting scythe. The curved steel blade is extra sharp, and when run along the inside edge of a pot, it loosens up the most stubborn root masses. This tool is extremely valuable for removing plants from pots that have an inwardly curved top rim. I use this tool as a last resort. When a root ball is so congested that potting or repotting is impossible, a few radial pulls away from the tree's trunk with this tool will loosen even a hopeless mass of roots. Caution is advised with this tool. Keep your other hand away from it while pulling and cutting. I even used this tool to scare away a burglar; so, take special care to treat it with respect. The top tools are an ordinary pair of chopsticks. These sticks are very convenient for probing into muddy areas of the root ball or packing in fresh soil. Keep them handy at all times.

A collection of pinching, grasping and tweezing tools is shown in **3–6**. Fingers are not as precise or as strong as these useful implements. At the top is a pair of stainless steel tweezers commonly found in the home medicine cabinet or first-aid kit. They can be used to pinch off scale insects, grab an errant string or thread, remove a tiny bud, or pick up tiny debris from the surface of a miniature bonsai pot. The second tool down is especially made for bending wire on small bonsai. Wire from the far side of a branch can be retrieved during wiring by reaching through with these small pliers. The curved tip is designed to kink the last ¼ inch of wire at the end of a branch, making it easier to secure to the branch. This tool's jaws are serrated to grab string, thread, wire, and bark in a variety of tasks. Just below are needle-nosed pliers with blue handles, common to household toolboxes. This tool will cut wire next to the swivel joint and perform the same functions as the bonsai wiring pliers above. Just below the blue-handled pliers is a pair of bonsai tweezers. One end is shaped like a spatula like those for root hooks (shown in **3–5**), and the other end is an elongated pair of tweezers with textured inner and outer surfaces for a good grip. I mostly use this tool for weeding bonsai. The long jaws reach deep to find dandelion roots and volunteer cherry trees planted by birds. The small tweezers second from the bottom of the photo have a set of tiny interlocking teeth which allow traction and grip. For rooting work, these tweezers are a headache since they need to have their tips

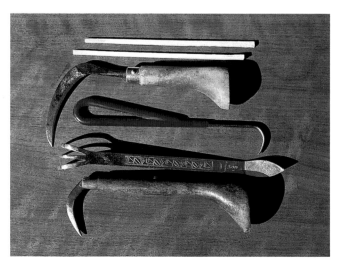

3–5

3–6

useful in manipulating wire, clamps, or screen. They will cut heavy-gauge wire. Their jaws are textured to grasp bark, twigs, and heavy roots that need convincing. The black tool next to the top tool is a readily available bonsai tool called a *jin*-maker. It's jaws are aggressively serrated and designed to grasp even the most slippery bark. One of the jaws is sharpened to provide a push type of carving tool to clean off the clinging remains of cambium debris. Its long handles give this tool a lot of force in small hands. I would recommend the *jin*-maker to anyone who has trouble ripping apart branches with bare hands. I don't use this tool often. The top pliers with the yellow handles are just a larger version of the pliers previously mentioned. The rubberized grips give this tool an advantage over others. Also, the jaws open a bit wider than most pliers. This tool is one of my favorites.

cleaned of clinging debris. For cleaning out an especially filthy trunk hollow, however, this tool is a welcome substitute for the steel tool just two tools above. The nonrusting alloy of these tweezers allows you to forget them out in the rain without concern. For a small investment, these tweezers will give you forty years of good service.

These pliers (see **3–7**) have special uses. The blue-handled pliers shown at the bottom of the photo have jaws that can be adjusted to open wide or narrow. I find that this is my favorite *jin*-making tool. I can adjust the size of the jaws to accommodate any size of branch or trunk. I can squeeze live branches prior to stripping the bark. I can grip, bend, and twist live branches to make them more interesting as *shari*. I can also grasp large trunks and small bark strips alike while forming *saba-miki*. The next two sets of pliers on the left, just above, are adjustable channel-lock pliers that I use together. I use the larger tool in my weaker left hand to support the work. In my right hand, the smaller pliers can sculpt live wood for use as driftwood later. Bend the wood while it's flexible and moist. After it dies and becomes brittle, I can treat it with lime sulfur for a nice driftwood gray effect. Just to their right is a common pair of vise-grip pliers. These are used to grasp a branch or trunk to stabilize it while you're doing other work. Often it is difficult to grip a branch during grafting or carving. This tool, once adjusted to the proper diameter, will continue to grasp your work until it is no longer needed. The regular pliers just above the vise grips are common to household toolboxes. They are

3–7

This family of tools cuts wire (see **3–8**). The bottom black bonsai wire cutters, made in Japan, are quite stout. They are 12 inches long and will easily cut 4-gauge copper wire. In an emergency, I was able to cut through a galvanized steel chain-link fence with them, but that's a long story. The Japanese wire cutters just above them are my favorite wire cutters. Made by Masakuni, they have an angled cutting tip that presents itself to the branch or wire in a practical fashion. The blue-handled pliers cut wire close to their swivel joint, and their needle-nosed jaws help twist the wire where needed. But they cannot cut wire off a branch—a major disadvantage of American-made wire cutters. The red-handled wire cutters are suitable for bonsai, but their pointed tips *almost* cut small wire next to a branch. If the wire is slightly embedded in the branch, as we all

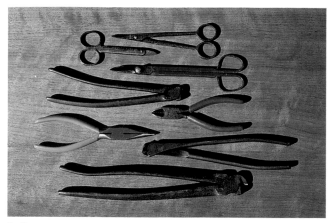

3—8

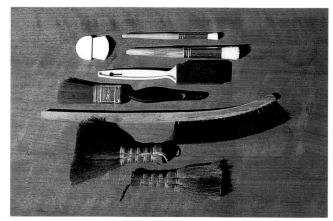

3—9

tend to let happen out of neglect, this tool will not do the job. The cutting tips are just not precise enough, and the short, curving handles make it extremely difficult to develop enough force.

I strongly recommend Japanese bonsai wire cutters, like the black wire cutters just above the blue-handled cutters. They're commonly available in bonsai nurseries. The curving handles are well designed. I wish wire cutters were made that had these wonderful handles on the offset cutting tip of the tool to the far right. This tool has a tip located at the extreme end. By raising your elbow a bit, you can make the wire enter the proper opening. These Japanese wire cutters are good all-around wire cutters which cut copper from 8 to 28 gauge. The red-handled tool second from the top of the photo is designed like branch trimmers, yet its cutting jaws have been beveled like those of wire cutters. I keep this tool handy because it is so useful. Often I don't know if a branch is going to be needed until after it has been wired. I'll try the branch in its new position and find that it isn't needed at all. With this red-handled tool, I can cut off the branch, wire and all. At the top left are black steel Japanese wire cutters designed for the smaller gauges used on miniature bonsai. They will cut from 16- to 28-gauge soft copper wire. They won't remove wire from a branch easily. At the top and to the right are the best all-around wire cutters for miniature bonsai. These cutters can cut branches as big as a chopstick, yet trim the tiniest of branchlets and twigs. They easily cut 18- to 28-gauge wire because their jaws are specially beveled to handle wire. When I work with one-handed bonsai, this is the tool I use most.

These are the brushes (see **3—9**). The bottom two are Japanese bonsai soil whisks. They are used to manipulate and contour the soil of bonsai and saikei during potting and repotting. They are well made and will last a long time. The bottom brush is 25 years old. The long curved brush is actually designed for applying wallpaper, but I find it useful as a miniature bonsai shelf cleaner. The 1½-inch brush just above that is a common latex paintbrush. It's useful for applying paint and stains to bonsai stands, smoothing off soil, and bleaching the growing bench. The foam disposable brush just above it is very practical when applying oil-based stains or varnishes to stands, bases, or homemade pots. At the upper left is a fine, soft brush normally used for applying make-up or blush. I use this for smoothing out the soil surfaces of miniature bonsai or small saikei. Its super-soft bristles give me the effect I need with small-grained soils where hands or fingers are clumsy and inadequate. On the upper right are two brushes originally designed for stencil painting. They make excellent accent brushes for miniature landscapes and miniature bonsai. Their bristles are stiff yet small and short for close work. They can even be used to clean and dress up miniature containers, apply bleach to bonsai tree trunks, and sweep off algae from the miniature growing bench.

These pruning saws (see **3—10**) are all small, compact, and lightweight. The saw on the lower right has very fine teeth and comes with its own red leather carrying case. It is my favorite for workshops and demonstrations. The black Japanese saw to its left is extremely fine. The cutting teeth are closely spaced, the pointed tip can reach into small crevices where the concave cutter cannot go. The largest saw immediately above is my favorite for collecting bonsai from the woods. It has coarse teeth and a stout handle you can easily pull. All these saws cut on the pull stroke rather than the push stroke. Even carpenter's saws in Japan cut on the pull stroke. Swedish saws cut on both the pull and push stroke, while American saws cut only on the push stroke. At the upper right is an old favorite I have used for thirty years. The teeth are extraordinarily long, yet still positioned close together. This saw is practically self-cleaning even on wet woods like willow, elm, and birch. To the upper left is a commonly available folding saw from Switzerland. The teeth are a bit coarse for bonsai work, but I enjoy it in the garden when working on my prebonsai stock that's growing in the ground.

3–10

This photo (**3–11**) shows a collection of carving tools. At left is a utility knife with a heavy metal handle that houses a number of disposable blades. When one blade gets dull, it can be simply thrown away and the handle opened to retrieve another fresh, unused blade. A thumb slide on the back exposes the desired amount of blade, a good safety feature. The heavy pocketknife to its right is another of my favorites. The blade is heavy yet sharp. It folds up into a convenient size for the pocket or tool roll. However, I have never had any use for all the gadgets in a Swiss army knife. The red-handled chisel is designed for use with a light leather or wooden mallet. For hollowing out oak trees or carving large amounts of wood away for *saba-miki*, this is the tool. Next is a common linoleum knife. Carpet layers like this knife's trimming edge as well. I like this tool when tracing cambium on larger specimens. The curve of the knife matches the outside curve of the trunk. The burr to its right is one example of a myriad of burrs available if you want to carve bonsai with motorized equipment. I've used such tools, but when I have the time, I prefer the peace and quiet of carving by hand.

Just above the burr is a pocketknife with disposable blades. These blades are sharp and ultra thin. So, do not attempt any scraping or bending as you carve; the blade will snap. A pocketknife is better. Next is an aluminum handle that holds a vast number of disposable blades. They are available from hobby shops where balsa wood carving is still encouraged. Every possible shape and size of blade is available for this handle. If you have a special carving need, they have the blade available. Again, disposable blades are brittle; so, watch the angle of your cut. Any twisting or turning of the blade will break it. The next three bamboo-handled carving tools are the tools I use most. Between these three, I find that I can accomplish most carving jobs. They are made of superior steel, carve easily, sharpen in a minute, hold their edge, and tolerate constant abuse like twisting, turning, and scraping. If you have only three carving tools, these should be the ones. Second from the right is a sushi knife. I like the quality of steel very much. It can be sharpened easily to a razor edge and used for grafting. The small pocketknife to the far right is a bit small for most purposes, but its two blades, one pointed and one blunt, are always sharp and available. This pocketknife is small and highly portable. It is always handy nearby.

3–11

Bonsai pots have relatively large drainage holes and should be covered with soffit screen or hardware cloth. You can buy plastic screen made in Japan at bonsai nurseries. Cut squares of 1/8-inch hardware cloth are shown on the lower right (see **3–12**). At the bottom of the photo is a small pair of tin snips or sheet-metal shears. These are appropriate for cutting squares of soffit screen. Just above, with the black handles, is an

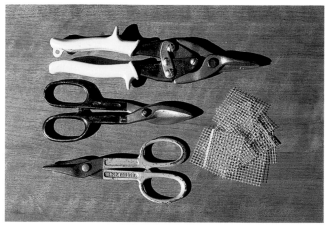

3–12

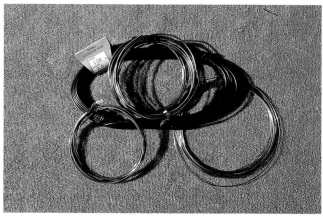

3–14

WIRING AND TRAINING DEVICES

This is an assortment of coils of solid, soft copper wire (3–14). The designation *soft* also means "annealed," which is the opposite of "tempered." Appropriate sizes of wire range from 4 gauge to 28 gauge (the larger the number, the thinner the wire). For miniature bonsai, obviously, the wire would be smaller—typically between 18 and 28 gauge. Aluminum wire is slightly easier to bend. For copper, use a wire about one-third the size of the branch you're trying to bend.

Other fastening and binding devices are shown in 3–15. Ordinary cotton string for binding plants to pots, pots to benches, rocks to pots, plants to rocks, and roots to pots is a toolbox essential. String is biodegradable and can rot away within the root ball. It's also not as harsh on roots or branches as copper, and it's certainly less expensive. I use it to temporarily stabilize a bonsai

ordinary pair of tin snips. At the top, the yellow-handled shears are part of a fancy set of three compound cutting shears. Red-handled ones, not shown, cut only to the right; blue-handled ones cut only to the left. The yellow-handled shears are designed to cut straight, and they're appropriate for bonsai use.

Wound sealers are necessary whenever the plant risks infection or dieback. A wound sealer must have at least one quality—the ability to seal off moisture and air from the newly pruned cut end. Shown in photo 3–13 are several suggestions, but possibilities are numerous. At the top left is petroleum jelly and to its right is a shallow tin of shoe polish. Below that and to the right are two bottles of glue, one general purpose, and another for wood. To the lower left, we see a tube of lip balm, a suitable wound sealer. At the very bottom in the green-topped container is commercially available Japanese bonsai wound sealer. Substitutes you could try include mud, tree sap, grafting wax, or mineral oil.

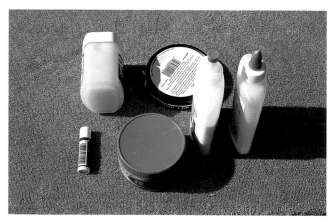

3–13

3–15

in a pot during transport.

The hard steel wire is common bailing wire. Use it wherever strength is necessary and rough appearance does not matter. The black thread on the upper left is useful for training weeping-style branches. A large weeping tree will have graceful arches in its branches. Bonsai made from the same tree will be upright, due to the shortness and light weight of its branches. Either use the thread to attach lead weights to the branch tips, or tie the branches down directly to the tree's surface roots or pot rim. At the far left is tape that sticks to itself but not to anything else. You can use this tape to repair broken branches, hold grafting scions to the host plant, tie roots to rocks, and shape root masses in preparation for exposed-root style trees. It only lasts one year. Ultraviolet light makes the tape brittle; so, it breaks and falls off within a year. I take advantage of this when growing bonsai material in the ground. If I wire a branch, I often forget it's there, and after a year, the branch becomes permanently scarred with circular wire marks. However, with this tape, if I forget to take it off, it doesn't matter. The two rolls of turquoise tape at the bottom are flexible plastic floral tape. The small size on the right is excellent for mending broken branches and protecting bark from wire damage. The larger size can be used for supporting field-grown azaleas against a training stake. This training method works well for weeping conifers, like weeping larch, Japanese green-mound juniper, weeping Atlantic cedar, and wiltoni juniper. This strong tape works well for bringing up a new apex on a tree. Retain the old stub of a top and tape the new top to it. The stubs will grow parallel to each other for one year, then you can prune out the dead stub.

Some time ago, I was asked to judge a bonsai show. I carefully reviewed suggested guidelines for judging. Of notice, among these guidelines was the need to deduct points or even disqualify trees not wired in accordance with established Japanese tradition. I thought about all my own trees out in the bonsai garden. Some branches were tied down to the bench. Others sported an array of shiny turnbuckles, fishing weights, and clamps. On some sensitive species, I had resorted to using plastic-coated insulated electrical wire rather than gamble with damage from bare copper.

My philosophy is that it's appropriate to use any method that works. But it's true that some so-called shortcuts eventually cause more work than if you had used traditional Japanese wiring techniques to begin with. However, if your method does not achieve the desired results, you still learned more about plant growth. Knowledge, experimentation, and observation are more important than a failed growing season on a single bonsai.

This pine tree (**3–16**) is gradually being bent with a bonsai clamp. The tough wood of high-altitude trees makes it impossible to utilize wire to bend trunks or larger branches. This clamp enables the grower to gradually bend the tree over time. Each day I water this tree, it reminds me to turn the screw a little more. It is amazing how loose the screw is after a few days' growth. I can hand tighten the clamp on Saturday and by Wednesday the branch has accommodated to the force enough that the clamp is actually loose again. Maintaining this force over an extended time enables the grower to bend branches that would be impossible to bend with wire. I realize that this would make an unacceptable tree to display in a show, but I have others that are ready. This is how I get them ready.

3–16

WATERING DEVICES AND PESTICIDE APPLICATORS

On the far right of photo **3–17** is an inexpensive plastic watering can. I keep this can filled with water at all times for my indoor plants. As plants indicate the need for moisture, I can water them immediately with room-temperature water that has been sitting, dissipating its chlorine and fluoride. A few drops of fertilizer can be added to the water so that nutrition is delivered to the

3–17

plants on a light, regular basis. This is far more health-ful than a sudden, massive dose of fertilizer splashed on a plant with cold, chlorinated water. On the far left is the outdoor equivalent, an inexpensive watering can.

In the middle of the photograph is one of my favorite all-around watering devices. This compressed-air sprayer waters my miniature bonsai, mists root hairs during transplanting, delivers a light dose of foliar fertilizer in the rain, and can be used to deliver vitamin B_1 to a struggling plant. It is portable. I can move it from the work table to the growing bench. I can use it to spray insecticides or fungicides or even take it in the woods to apply antidesiccant to a potential bonsai spec-imen before digging.

Other simple watering devices to consider are in **3–18**. At the far left is a popular hose-end nozzle de-signed to deliver a predictable soft spray of water. The trigger is adjustable to allow the grower to blast away with a large volume of water for plants in the ground or a small volume for potted bonsai. The sprayer has an optional quick-release mechanism for ease in switching to other watering devices, such as a broadcast sprin-kler. At the bottom of the photo is a curious-looking brass device known as a siphon. Simply screw the metal end into your hose bib, and then dangle the rubber end into a large bucket. Your regular garden hose can then be hooked up to the other end of the brass device. Once this is connected, add diluted liquid fertilizer to the bucket to convert your garden hose into a fertilizing wand. It works equally well for all containerized plants. Due to the decreased flow of water, this method is not appropriate for lawns or shrubbery, but I can fertilize over 1,000 bonsai in less than twenty minutes with this device. At the top is a commonly available nozzle de-signed to deliver a heavy mist. Screwed onto the end of

a garden hose, you can safely water miniature bonsai without knocking them over with the force of the spray. These nozzles are available in many types, ranging from a super-fine mist all the way to a drenching spray, and everything in between. Just near the top is a green-handled bonsai nozzle. Several companies now make these nozzles which copy the fine spray obtained from a small copper watering can. With the water on high pressure you can direct a fine spray toward the bonsai from a distance of 12 feet or more. This spray is ideal for hot summer mornings when everything is going to bake by noon. On the other hand, this nozzle equipped with a shutoff valve (similar to the aluminum one on the lower right) can duplicate the nice, small arch of water that's wonderful for watering individual bonsai. Remember to point the nozzle up, and let the water spill down from the air above the plant. Do not attempt to point the spray directly down toward the bonsai or you'll wash away soil from the pots. At the right is a simple soaking sprinkler that works well to drench bonsai material in the ground. There's a hole in the aluminum casting that will allow you to nail this sprin-kler head to a shelf or fence post for specific watering tasks.

The pistol type of hose nozzle in the center of photo **3–18** I use to bare root bonsai material. I carry the plant onto the lawn and direct the blast of water toward the muddy root ball until the water runs clear. Then I add bonsai soil and know that the plant will thrive. The nozzle above it serves the same purpose. Just to the right of the red-handled nozzle is a typical watering device that enables you to operate a bonsai nozzle and a sprinkler at the same time. Each side has its own turn-off valve so that you can operate each independently or

3–18

together. The brass quick-release near the center right of this photo is typical of metal and plastic fittings available to make your watering tasks easier. Its plastic equivalent is at the hose end of the red watering gun. Last, the perfectly round silver and blue watering rose found near the bottom is my favorite nozzle to water container stock that's not yet in bonsai pots. It emits a dense stream of water that floods 1-, 2-, 3-, and 5-gallon containers rapidly. I can water hundreds of plants in a few minutes with this device. If I run the sprinkler over the tops of the same containers, the task takes four times as long and wastes a tremendous amount of water.

THE WORK AREA

Turntables

A turntable (3–19) should be located at the center of your working surface. It's frustrating to work on a tree without one. As you prune, wire, or try to view the tree, you can rotate the turntable this way and that. Without the benefit of the turntable, your pot and tree will be scuffed around the work surface. This not only mars the table's finish, but it tends to dislodge the freshly planted bonsai from its pot. With a turntable, you can view all sides of the planting. This turntable, made in Japan, has a heavy cast-iron base, and the turning surface is made of thick, laminated wood with a marine type of glue that resists moisture. A turn screw on the right side prevents unnecessary rotation. When you tighten this screw, the bonsai will not turn while you

wire or trim. To rotate the tree, simply loosen this screw with your fingers and the turntable easily pivots in both directions.

This turntable (3–20) is made of Alaskan red cedar with a nonslip rubber mat on top. The base is finely jointed together. Underneath the turntable (3–21), the center dowel turns easily on a white collar of resin, and in each corner of the base are small swivels that slow the rotating action of the upper round disk. The turntable does not rotate when you apply light pressure on the tree during wiring it, but will easily move when desired.

3–20

3–21

3–19

Necessaries

The work table should also have these items close by—bins of soil, a tool drawer, spools of wire, sharpening stones, garbage can, lubricants, and cleanup equipment. If these items are readily available, your work will progress easily. You'll enjoy training bonsai more, and your trees will have a greater chance of survival. It's frustrating, in the middle of a project, to have to run to the garage to look for a tool. It's even more exasperating to stop during root pruning to look for the vitamin B_1 in the garden shed. If you assemble all these items in advance, in a central location, your work will go smoothly.

Growing Bench

The growing bench should be high enough to allow easy access for maintenance of your trees. About 40 inches high seems adequate for a nice display as well. Try to select a location suitable for most of your trees. I recommend morning sun rather than afternoon, because that eliminates the danger of excess summer ultraviolet light. Bonsai grow better when rotated and moved around according to the seasons. But if your primary growing bench accommodates most of your trees, you'll find it most convenient. Create a neutral background for display purposes; that's an integral part of the art. It will also help you make design and development decisions.

Construction of the growing bench can be as varied as the bonsai displayed on top. I favor cedar, redwood, or pressure-treated lumber. The surface should drain extremely well, and slats of wood no wider than 4 inches with a generous gap between them work best. Moisture expands wood considerably; so, do not construct a shelf with tiny cracks between individual boards. Slant the entire shelf slightly away from the viewer to allow additional drainage and make the shelf seem slightly higher. A growing bench you can look down on will appear low; a bench viewed from the edge will appear taller and will accentuate the finer qualities of your designs. In addition, it is preferable to drain excess water toward the back of the shelf rather than to have it pour forward onto your shoes.

To help keep the bench insect and disease free, rest each leg in a can of water. The leg should be raised out of the water using a nail driven into its bottom (see **8—5** in chapter 8). Crawling insects cannot penetrate this simple barrier. Also see the insect section of chapter 8.

Every summer, clear off your growing bench and apply half-strength bleach solution to all surfaces. Allow the liquid to penetrate the wood for about an hour, and then rinse with clear water. Two weeks later, you may want to apply a wood preservative or Danish oil to restore the natural brown wood color. Bleach is a powerful disinfectant and will help you get through the fall, winter, and spring without disease.

Protection from Pests

For miniature bonsai, common garden pests can wreak havoc in just one morning's activity. Protect your tiny trees against squirrels, chipmunks, birds, mice, and deer.

Netting, screening, or some enclosure may be necessary to protect miniature bonsai. Shade cloth can double as screening against blue jays or crows. The work area's close proximity to the living area may discourage deer, raccoons, opossum, or beaver. Nevertheless, I have armed myself with a broomstick to defend my trees from the jaws of hungry raccoons. My bonsai nursery was once located downtown in a city of over a million people. To cut down on vandalism, I purchased a guard dog to protect my trees. I heard the suspicious breaking of a pot early one morning and ran to the bedroom window to observe my guard dog prancing proudly around the yard with one of my bonsai in his mouth, stopping once in a while to shake the tree as if it were a rat. Pests come in all sizes and shapes. Your growing bench must serve as a protective device from the kinds of damage you might be subjected to in your local area.

SOIL

Stainless steel soil screens, shown here in a variety of sizes (**3—22**), imported from Japan, can be useful. The circular screen holders accommodate any of the various screen mesh sizes shown. Five different mesh sizes are available in the removable screen inserts, ranging from ³⁄₃₂ inch up to ³⁄₁₆ inch. These two sizes are roughly the sizes of common window screen at the smallest and soffit hardware cloth at the largest. Basically, all you do is sort the sizes of soil particles to use. For most bonsai purposes, a particle size between ³⁄₃₂ and ¹⁄₈ inch in diameter is suitable. For miniature bonsai purposes, a smaller size is better, to increase moisture retention. For a detailed explanation of bonsai soil, see chapter 6.

3–22

3–23

GROWING CONTAINERS

As a child I discovered that growing containers could be made out of walnut shells, thimbles, pot pie tins, tuna fish cans, small wooden bowls, automotive parts, match boxes, and acorn shells. You'll find a wild flower in chapter 5 planted in the tiny cap of an acorn. Students have used *sake* cups, small decorated bowls, brake drums, teacups, saucers, cloisonné, knickknacks, netsuke, and *sashimi* trays, and even napkin rings. Any container, no matter what size, shape, or color, can be planted with some kind of bonsai. Sometimes the plant will determine the pot. Other times, you'll find a special container you want to utilize, but you want to use the container to its best advantage.

These pages show a small collection of miniature bonsai pots in a wide variety of sizes, textures, colors, shapes, and styles. Along with each photo, I suggest what could complement the container. In chapter 7, we'll take some of these pots and match them with plant material in a workshop setting.

For students on a budget or for trees that do not warrant a more expensive container, this plastic pot (**3–23**) may be a great choice. They cost between $1 and $2 and provide a better visual display than nonbonsai plastic nursery pot counterparts. This container makes a nice training pot. Its brown earth tone would complement a fairly stout pine tree or other conifer. A very young plant has plenty of room to grow.

This pot (**3–24**) is the shiny equivalent of the pot just above. It is a solid blue plastic pot in a pleasing round shape. Once planted, it doesn't look too bad. The deep blue color complements most maples, cotoneaster, pyracantha, and other red-leaved bonsai youngsters. Leaves in yellow or orange hues look better in creamier

3–24

colors than this blue.

Compare this gray blue (**3–25**) with the previous container. A mottled red orange leaf, such as the trident maple, looks nice in this subtle blue. This is a fairly large miniature bonsai container, 5 inches across. Plant a 3-year-old Japanese maple in this pot. The gently undulating curves of the maple in its natural form complement the gentle curves of this oval container.

The container shown in **3–26** is quite small, only 1½ inches wide. Its precision cloisonné enamel glaze and its bright brass edge require a planting of equal exactitude. Try a *hokkaido* elm, cotoneaster microphylla, or clump of bloodgrass in this sharp-looking pot. Containers like this need to have drainage holes drilled in them. You can do this with a general-purpose drill bit. And the soft brass can be easily penetrated with cutting oil and a metal-cutting drill bit at slow speed.

3-25

3-26

3-27

This black glazed container (3–27) will house a variety of trees well. The white birch bark contrasts nicely with the shiny dark glaze. The creamy barks of elm, alder, hornbeam, or beech will look striking. The fall color of deciduous conifers is also complemented by this dark, shiny glaze. Try the upright form of larch, tamarix, or deciduous cypress in this pot.

The brown glaze automatically indicates that a conifer would look best in this pot (3–28). The shape of the container indicates *bunjin*. The esoteric literati style looks best in these shallow, round pots. Try a young, but picturesque alpine fir, a mountain hemlock, or a sparse, layered juniper. The plant should be three times as tall as the container is wide. It should be light, airy, and gently undulating in its trunk form.

This blue glaze indicates that a colorful deciduous tree would look best in it (3–29). The shape of the pot suggests that the plant's rootage should be an object of focus. Try a miniature rock planting or root-over-rock style in this pot, and you'll find these styles complement the container's flared edges. This need not be an older tree. A 3- to 5-year-old crab apple with its trunk wedged into a rock crevice would be ideal.

This elegant cascade pot (3–30) needs a fairly dark leaf color to complement its rich blue and black tones. A cascading plum or cherry would be nice. Experiment with other flowering species such as red quince, *Prunus mume*, apricot, myrtle, or manzanita.

The creamy quality of this blue glaze makes the pot shown in 3–31 a prime candidate for the mottled colors of vine maple, trident maple, copper beech, and wild plum. The decorative pattern in the center of the container suggests flowers, twisted branches, and an undulating trunk style, such as *moyogi*.

3-28

3–29

3–30

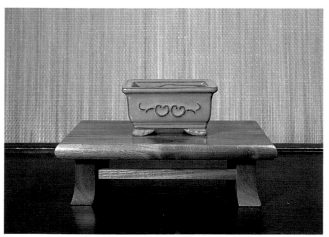

3–31

The flared edge of this earth brown container (**3–32**) suggests a root-exposed conifer, such as an alpine juniper or hardy pine. By placing a few small angular rocks among the roots, it will appear that the tree is growing in a highly eroded area.

The small raised dots around the perimeter of this dark brown container (**3–33**) are designed to imitate the fastenings of a Japanese drum. The conifer placed in this pot should be angularly curved, rather than gently curved in the typical *bunjin* style. When the trunk changes direction, it should be sudden, not gradual. The force of nature's hardships should be evident here as suggested by the tightness and force of the drum's shape.

This brick red cascade pot (**3–34**) requires a conifer with reddish brown bark that tumbles down one side. Look for delicately shaped cypress, cedar, chamaecyparis, juniper, or hemlock to grace this well-decorated container. The light quality of the calligraphy and the grass design suggest a dry landscape; so, it's best to utilize sparse foliage on your plant. A heavy, bushy, or dense tree would be internally inconsistent with the shape, character, and spirit of this container.

The bold blue of the cascade pot (**3–35**) makes it a natural choice for a leaning cherry, dangling quince, or informal cascade mum. Remember to allow the lowest branch on these trees to extend well below the bottom of the container. A cascade pot must have a fairly tall stand to accommodate this lowest foliage; otherwise, a semicascade pot is more appropriate. See chapter 4.

The container in **3–36** is an exquisite, signed piece from Japan. The irregularity of the glaze is not accidental. The earth brown colors of the base, which progress to the living colors of yellow and green, display a natural progression from mineral to organic. Even the light blue top edge suggests culmination as the sky. A special plant of historic importance would complement this special container. Try an old rose or camellia cascading over one edge or perhaps a pomegranate. An old, bent-over pyracantha could suggest an apple tree with its tiny, similarly shaped blossoms followed by red fruit.

I once picked up an empty pot that was for sale and found that its price tag was nearly half a million dollars. Fortunately, I was able to return the container to its stand before too much blood had drained from my arms or face so that the pot was actually not in any serious danger. The pot shown in **3–37** is only about 1½ inches wide, but it carries a surprising price tag. I may plant something in it someday, or I may not. I might consider an old specimen of corokia cotoneaster.

3–32

3–33

3–34

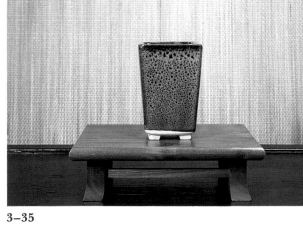

3–35

3–36

3–37

The multipastel colors of blue and gray in the container shown in **3–38** make it an ideal pot for the yellows and oranges of native flowering trees. Try the unusual nine bark, choke cherry, wild rose, huckleberry, or bearberry. A fairly stout trunk and angled branches would complement the unusual eight-sided design of this pot. The inside turn of the rim on this design makes transplanting difficult; so, repot your tree every year without fail and avoid trees with invasive, aggressive roots, such as elm, birch, or willow.

The delicate painting on the side of the container in **3–39** is hand drawn and continuous around the circumference. Its colors are tan, beige, and dark brown. I have never wanted to plant anything in this pot due to its exquisite design; however, I suppose if I ever found just the right tree, I might consider it. I would look for a dark plum or copper beech. Some purple and brown varieties of lace-leaf Japanese maple would look nice, but it would have to be a special tree indeed.

I first became aware of the custom of potters signing their containers when I was studying in Japan. Containers produced from molds were not as attractive to my eye, and I was drawn toward the irregularity of some shapes and glazes. I soon discovered that I was being drawn toward the signature pieces. The pot in **3–40** is a good example. There's not another exactly like it anywhere, because it's handmade and signed by its creator. I would plant a flowering cherry, apricot, or almond in this excellent miniature bonsai container.

The unusual gold design on an otherwise ordinary brown pot makes this container noticeable (**3–41**). A slanting style miniature conifer would look well planted in it. By placing the tree on the right side of the pot, you can complement the floral pattern on the left. A classic pine tree shape would look best.

When I came across this design (**3–42**), I simply had to have it. Frankly, I have not ever seen anything like it before, and I've never tried to plant anything in this pot. I guess it would be difficult to transplant a tree from a design like this because of its overhanging inner rim. A well-designed *bunjin* reaching up high and leaning slightly to one side would probably be the best planting for this pot.

The multishades of white and blue in this octagon-shaped, shallow pot (**3–43**) make it ideal for any fat-trunked, broom style of deciduous tree. Try an old rosemary bush, *seiju* elm, cotoneaster, crab apple, or azalea. Any plant that grows wider than it does tall will look good in a container of this shape. Dwarf rhododendrons, myrtle, mountain mahogany, buttonwood,

3–38

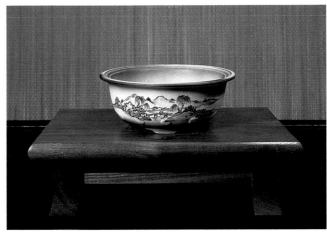

3–39

3–40

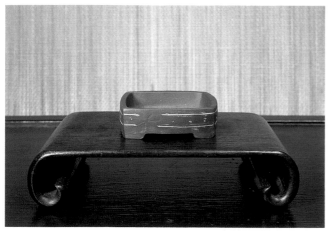

3—41

3—42

3—43

or sage would do equally well. If your planting looks better from a different angle than your original idea, just turn the pot.

The pot in **3—44** is perhaps the world's smallest saikei tray. It is actually a pleasing oval shape with a nice rounded rim just like the 40-inch trays commonly employed for larger miniature landscape use. However, this pot is only 2 inches long, a formidable planting task for the bonsai artist wanting to combine miniature bonsai and saikei. Can you imagine a forest of ¼-inch tall trees among ½-inch tall "boulders" in this pot?

The pot in **3—45** is not a classic *bunjin* shape. Notice that the top edge of the pot is flared outward, instead of inward. This indicates that a root or rock presence is best. A miniature rock planting of little gem spruce would be ideal. Similarly, any genetic dwarf conifer such as pixie pine, waconda spruce, andelyensis cypress, dwarf *hinoki* cypress, or mountain hemlock would look great. An interesting rock would make the planting superior.

The unusually detailed reddish brown cascade pot in **3—46** is an excellent example of the potter's art. It is so fine and detailed that, without a description of its size, you would think it to be a fairly large pot. Actually, it is only 1¾ inches tall. If you decide to plant a pot like this, use a cascading bearberry, manzanita, or red-barked juniper to show off the rich, golden brown and red brick colors in the clay.

The unusual symmetrical raised design of the pot in **3—47** is what attracted me to it. Its unique oval design is rarely seen, although some very old Chinese containers exhibit this form. This shape may be older than China; it's similar to ancient Greek or Egyptian motifs. Plant an old specimen of pine in this pot. Use the classic *moyogi* style with branches radiating outside the gentle curves of its trunk to complement the curves of this unusual oval, earth brown container.

What we have seen here are but a few of the hundreds of styles, colors, and shapes of miniature bonsai containers available. Growers attracted to the small size of miniature bonsai can't help but be attracted to the diminutive size of the containers as well. Indeed, if you meet a specialist in miniature bonsai, you've probably met a collector of miniature pots as well. They're fun to accumulate, generally less expensive than their larger counterparts, widely available, and they take up little room in the china cabinet.

3–44

3–45

3–46

3–47

4

DESIGN &
DEVELOPMENT

ELEMENTS OF STYLE

Individual style or thought, a characteristic mode of expression, is the basis for *bunjinji*. Scholars from the Lingnan School in China were allowed to express individual styles as they demonstrated the mastery of bonsai art. These signature pieces were the first accepted and recognizable signs of individuality in a heretofore highly structured intellectual society. Unknowingly, we all have our own individual style. It is possible to leaf through a bonsai magazine and identify the designer of a tree without reading the caption under the photograph. I can go to a local show and look at some trees and immediately identify their owners just by looking at the style. This is a compliment, to the artist, curator, and museum, that a work of art is easily identified by its style alone. I think every artist eventually finds an individual style that suits him or her.

Periodic style could be likened to the phases that an artist goes through. We hear of Picasso's blue period, Renoir's classic period, or Van Gogh's Oriental period. The bonsai I create today are certainly different from those I developed just five years ago. Perhaps they are better, perhaps not, but for me the change was subtle and gradual. I look at photos of my earlier work and realize how different it truly was. For now, I am comfortable with the present period I am engaged in. Perhaps, in five more years, I'll look back at what I've created in wonder or disapproval. I don't know. But it does not matter, does it? For the present, we can enjoy creating bonsai that suit us best. For the moment.

In Japan, student apprentices often imitated the style of the master. While students can be encouraged to express themselves in projects, a bonsai beginner does not have as many options as an experienced grower. Many beginners are fearful, and they cannot draw from experience. So, their first projects often reflect the opinions of the particular school. Bonsai has schools of thought, just like other creative disciplines.

Consider the idea of the national style of Japan or China in relation to bonsai. Yet there is no distinctive Swiss or English bonsai design. That's because the styles of their native landscapes have not yet become incorporated into accepted bonsai design modes. Perhaps it will happen. National styles usually evolve over centuries. Bonsai was introduced to Europe just a hundred years ago, but national style differences appear to be developing. These are not yet well defined, but observe how the oak, hawthorn, and hedge maple are styled in England, a country known for its Sherwood Forest, rocky moors, and hunting fields. Compare this with the Swiss treatment of their native mugho pine from the Alps. How could there not be a difference?

Let's consider three important elements of style—consistency, asymmetry, and interest. Good design, or indeed good art, is hard to define. These three attributes distinguish good style from random renderings. Examine each element, and you'll have a better understanding of how to dig deep within yourself to create art that satisfies you as a designer and that reflects your inner self.

Consistency

Is it just me or does lack of consistency with what's found in nature bother you as well? I look at a gorgeous picture of a *shimpaku* juniper on a Japanese bonsai calendar. Its trunk is twisted and contorted every way imaginable. Its foliage is trimmed meticulously by hand. Every errant bud is pinched off to create thick and beautiful, lush green clouds of dense needles. On the soil surface a carefully manicured lawn of beautiful moss braces the slightly exposed rootage. What's wrong with this picture? Every time I go to the woods to find an embattled, twisted juniper, its foliage is consistent with its branches and trunk. And no lush moss is anywhere to be seen. I cannot presume to criticize famous bonsai examples, but I would love to have the chance to style one of those old 500-year-old junipers into a vision consistent with what I personally observe in the wilderness. Consistency. If your lowest and largest branch angles up from the trunk at 10 degrees above the horizontal plane, then all the branches should do the same. They experience the same snow, frost, wind, and summer heat; so, they should look similar. Avoid arranging your branches like flowers in *ikebana*; there is little similarity between these two art forms. Empty space is often abhorred in arranging flowers. Vacant areas on a bonsai when explained by ambient weather around your tree can indicate consistency of style.

Asymmetry

Perhaps this should be expressed as lack of symmetry. Early English *topiary* is the horizontal art of creating plant material into fanciful shapes and figures by judicious pruning. Boxwood hedges are formed into mazes. Camellias become elephant shapes, and ivy draped over wire forms resembles porticoes and statuary. Bonsai gets its inspiration from nature and its inherent forces. It is unlikely that you'll run across wild cedar that looks like a series of stacked globes on a stick.

It is just as unlikely that topiary techniques would be appropriate for bonsai design. Actually it is difficult to find this perfect symmetry in nature. We do find it at the atomic level; in the alternate, opposite, or whorl pattern of leaves; or in the bilateral symmetry of animals. But the hydrotropic, heliotropic, and geotropic needs of plants necessarily create irregular growth patterns. Even the most calm and splendid pasture tree leans slightly in one direction. One branch is always the longest, and the apex is positioned slightly to one side, usually the sunny side. Asymmetry is an integral part of plant growth. Imposed symmetry suggests something human-made or manufactured. Good design, however, seems to strike a balance, weighing components of display for the eye; balancing light and dark, rough and smooth, vertical and horizontal. But this balance is not fabricated, mirrored, or symmetrical. Bonsai is never planted in the center of the pot. The tree is never as wide as it is tall. Two branches are never the same height, length, or diameter. Bonsai rules come from a teacher's effort to guide the frightened student. These rules are meant to help, not stultify or constrain.

Interest

This element is the easiest to define or describe, but it's the hardest to create. Interest is that factor or motif that draws your eye. It's what can make your design extraordinary or remarkable. Interest may be an aspect of incongruity that elevates your style above the ordinary. If one followed all the rules for creating a formal upright bonsai, for example, you'd create a boring tree. But without these same parameters, a formal upright tree could not be formed at all. If ten formal upright trees were placed side by side in a show, which would draw the most interest? Which tree, within the confines of accepted standards, would manage to excel and draw the viewer's attention? The tree that does this possesses interest and is a better design. It might just be an unusual carving job on the *saba-miki*. Perhaps it's due to the extreme downward slant of the branches. Sometimes it's the pure communication of calm or deep primeval forest that attracts the eye. In any case, try to develop this design attribute. If your tree is slightly embattled, ask yourself these questions: Would it be more or less interesting to exaggerate the tree's hardships? Would a stronger visual statement be possible by adding more *shari*? Be aware of the statement you are trying to make. If you can clarify that statement, then do it. In design, a clear statement is superior to a vague whisper.

JIN, SHARI, AND *SABA-MIKI*

Jin is a god or deity in Japan, and this word is often used to describe the intentional creation of dead wood on bonsai design. Viewing *jin* reminds the Japanese of the power of the gods through the physical evidence found in nature as dead wood on a living tree. In bonsai horticultural vernacular specifically, the dead top of a tree is labeled *jin*, a dead branch *shari*, and the dead portion of a trunk *saba-miki*. These may be presented in a design in many combinations as well as in many different so-called styles of trees. A formal upright tree, for example, might have just a dead top, or *jin*. A slanting style might have none of the three dead elements. A broom-style oak tree might have a huge *saba-miki*. Driftwood style normally has all three elements.

The fine old tree in **4–1** has had its top dried out by the prevailing wind and lack of rainfall. We can duplicate this effect on our bonsai, if this is the effect we desire. It is not necessary. All too often we use this

4–1

4—2

4-3

FIVE BASIC STYLES

In bonsai books you'll find descriptions of as many as 60 bonsai styles, including several esoteric designs not often seen. But there are only a certain number of ways that a trunk can be curved, which appear here as five basic styles. How the trunk line moves is the sole basis for this categorization. This does not consider the tree's species, environment, or growth characteristics. In the world of miniature bonsai, trunk movement is difficult indeed. In just 3 inches, try to accomplish three bends on the trunk of a pine tree. What follows is a simplification of bonsai design that's appropriate for miniature bonsai, the focus of this book.

Formal Upright Style—*Chokkan*
This style (**4–4**) is defined by its straight, vertical trunk. The apex is positioned directly over the root buttress. There is no side-to-side wavering of the trunk line. This

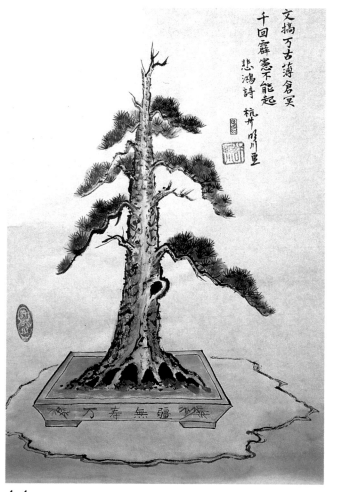

technique to shorten a tree that's too tall, forgetting the design implications of such a decision. If the top looks like this, then what should the branches look like? In an environment harsh enough to desiccate the top of a tree, we often find *shari* and *saba-miki* as well (see **4–2**). In forests with plenty of moisture and the absence of a strong prevailing wind, these dead areas are not present (see **4–3**). Notice, we now have three legitimate models for forming the design of the formal upright style. Keep in mind *jin*, *shari*, and *saba-miki* as you consider the five major bonsai styles. The appearance of dead wood on a bonsai does not determine the style. It only suggests the environmental conditions under which the tree is growing.

4-4

style may be lush or arid, alpine or desert. Branch placement is consistent. The root buttress is visible and dominant, and growth always proceeds from bottom to top, thereby communicating strong apical dominance in its horticulture. This tree might be the lone sentinel on a rock plateau or one of thousands like it deep in the rain forest. The trunk line alone defines the style.

Informal Upright Style—*Moyogi*
Again, the trunk line determines this style (**4–5**). The tree, against mild adversity, undulates to and fro in an effort to regain apical dominance. Eventually the apex rests comfortably directly over the root buttress below. This style offers a feeling of balance. Adversity appears overcome and the tree sits proudly displaying its war ribbons. This is the most popular style. It is often seen as the backdrop for ancient Noh plays. It is the most popular style seen in the android Data's quarters on the television series "Star Trek: The Next Generation."

4–6

4–5

Slanting Style—*Shakkan*
Environmental adversity makes it impossible for the apex of this tree to recover from its bent posture (**4–6**). The top of this moderately stressed tree is located to one side of the root buttress. This bonsai may be curved, straight, or quite angular. It is often windswept as seen in Miyagi's tree, popularized in the movie *Karate Kid II*. Strong roots help stabilize this tree, without which it can appear in danger of falling down.

Semicascade Style—*Han-Kengai*
This tree (**4–7A**), due to erosion or environmental stress, has chosen an interesting response. The apex, normally a strong leader on trees of this species, has deferred to a lower branch which thrives in comparative calm. Growth hormones still favor the upright growth habits of the species, but the lowest branch gets larger due to its advantageous position. Plant this bonsai in a round or square pot that's as wide as it is tall. The extra height of this semicascade container will

accommodate the lower large branches of the tree.

The long lower branch of this tree (**4–7B**) epitomizes the semicascade style. The blue container has just enough height to raise the foliage above the bench level. I designed this with my wife. It is a 41 × 20-inch needlepoint work, depicting a *Prunus mume* surrounded by decorative Japanese fans and Greek key borderwork. I completed the preparation of the canvas in one all-night work session, but my wife Susan's needlework took two years to complete.

4–8

4–7A

4–7B

Cascade Style—*Kengai*

Exaggerate the semicascade style and you produce the cascade style (**4–8**). Indeed, this is often how their bonsai equivalents are grown, just as they would grow in nature. If a semicascade were grown for an extended period of time, I am sure you can visualize what would happen. The same forces that created the long, lowest branch would cause it to extend so that a tall container would be necessary to keep its tip off the table or growing bench. This is why cascade pots were designed to allow the lowest branch to extend below the tall pot. An additional stand is necessary for display purposes.

Avoid the common pitfall: do not create a cascading bonsai by bending the trunk down. Form a small tree independent of the cascading lower branch for best results. After all, this is the way they develop in nature when growing on a windswept rock ledge.

OTHER STYLES

The five basic styles—*chokkan*, *moyogi*, *shakkan*, *han-kengai*, and *kengai*—constitute the full range of trunk movement in a tree. Other styles are named because of other factors. The windswept style, for example, is usually nothing more than a slanting style with all branches facing in one direction. A root-over-rock style only describes the relationship between a tree's roots and the rock it clasps; the tree could still maintain an informal upright style. We have previously discussed the possibility of *jin* on bonsai. So-called driftwood style is simply a slanted style converted into a windswept style, partially killed to form driftwood style. The myriad styles listed here are actually named varieties of specimen trees which occur in nature.

Single Tree Styles

Formal Upright—*Chokkan*

Informal Upright—*Moyogi* or *Tachiki*

Slanting—*Shakkan*

Semicascade—*Han-Kengai*

Formal Cascade—*Kengai*

Informal Cascade—*Kengai*

Bunjin, *Literati*, or *Bunjinji*

Elongated—*Goza Kake*

Drawings shown on these pages (58 to 63) illustrate additional styles—the elongated (*goza kake*), weeping (*shidare* or *zukuri*), windswept (*fukinagashi*), coiled (*bankan*), twisted (*nejikan*), knobby trunk (*kobukan*), hollow trunk (*sabakan*), split trunk (*saba-miki*), exposed root (*ne agari*), driftwood (*shara-miki* or *sara-miki*), peeled bark (*sharikan*), rock-grown (*ishitsuke* or *ishi zuki*), broom (*hoki dachi* or *hoki zukuri*), octopus (*tako zukuri*), buds or perennials (*shitakusa*), root-over-rock (*sekijojo* or *sekijoju*), sprout (*miyama kirishima* or *kabudachi*), grass planting (*kusamomo*), raft (*ikadabuki*), double trunk (*sokan*), triple trunk (*tosho*), and root-connected (*netsunari*).

In addition, the *bunjin*, *literati*, or *bunjinji* style listed above may be indefinite and variable. Typically, this elegant form has a slightly slanting trunk with branches and foliage developed only at the crown. Usually practiced by old bonsai masters, this style sometimes imitates Chinese calligraphy.

Weeping—*Shidare* or *Zukuri*

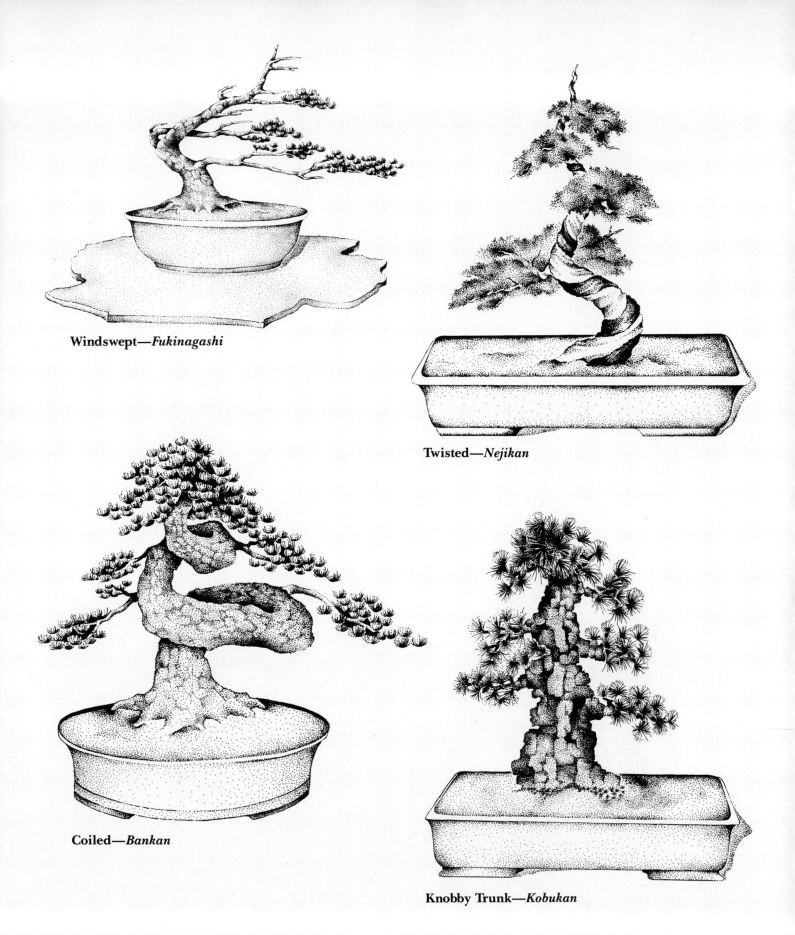

Windswept—*Fukinagashi*

Twisted—*Nejikan*

Coiled—*Bankan*

Knobby Trunk—*Kobukan*

Hollow Trunk—*Sabakan*

Exposed Root—*Ne Agari*

Driftwood—*Shara-miki* or *Sara-miki*

Split Trunk—*Saba-miki*

Peeled Bark—*Sharikan*

Broom—*Hoki Dachi* **or** *Hoki Zukuri*

Rock-Grown—*Ishitsuke* **or** *Ishi Zuki*

Octopus—*Tako Zukuri*

Buds or Perennials—*Shitakusa*

Sprout—*Miyama Kirishima* or *Kabudachi*

Root-Connected—*Netsunari*

Grass Planting—*Kusamomo*

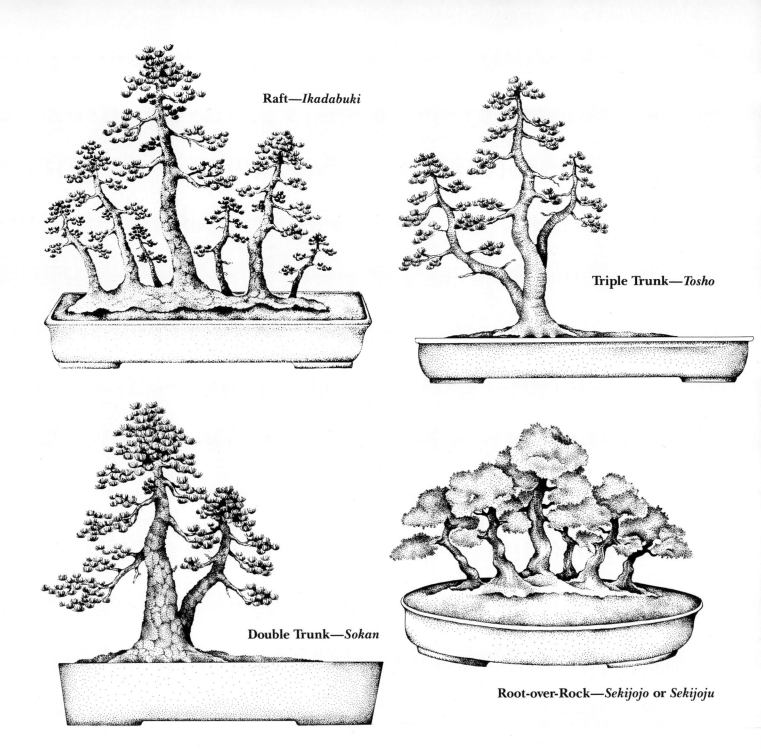

Raft—*Ikadabuki*

Triple Trunk—*Tosho*

Double Trunk—*Sokan*

Root-over-Rock—*Sekijojo* or *Sekijoju*

Multiple Tree Styles

Two Tree—*So Ju* or *So-ju*

Three Tree—*Sambon Yose*

Five Tree—*Gohon Yose*

Seven Tree—*Nanahon Yose*

Nine Tree—*Kyuhon Yose*

Group Planting—*Yose Uye* or *Yose Ue*

Miniature Landscape—*Saikei*

Clustered—*Tsukami Yose*

Natural—*Yoma Yori* or *Yoma Yose*

Fallen Cone—*Yama Yori*

Hundred Tree—*Yama Yori*

Allow these styles to stimulate your interest in varying your bonsai designs. (For more detailed discussion of these styles see my book *The Bonsai Workshop*, Sterling Publishing Co., 1994.) Your creativity can work wonders in producing and developing a bonsai that you can be proud of. Get out into nature and observe these styles firsthand. Look closely at how trees cling to rocks (**4–10**). What does a root buttress look like in an arid area (**4–11**)? Can you duplicate that root buttress in a bonsai pot (**4–12**)?

4–10

4–9

4–11

4–12

DESIGN DEVELOPMENT OVER TIME

Most people have difficulty understanding that bonsai are never finished. They see a bonsai demonstration. At the end, the artist explains that the tree is not finished. You see beautiful pictures of bonsai in books. You see fabulous photographs in magazines, journals, calendars, and posters. They are not finished yet. Many of these masterpieces are still evolving years after they were originally photographed. Their owners constantly strive for perfection. Their original design years before is but a photographic memory. Many beginners are disappointed to learn their bonsai isn't finished yet. "But I've been working on it for over two hours!" one of my students said.

Design development cannot be accomplished in a few hours. It is quite likely that some trees will be unable to reach their design potential for many years. Careful observation of nature and patience are important. Too often a *shari* is sharpened to look like a popsicle stick rubbed on the sidewalk. Detail plays an important part in overall appearance. Study dead branches in nature (**4–13**). *Shari* are complex; they will challenge your sculptural skills. You're not just dealing with a dead branch. *Shari* requires more time and attention than a few swipes with your pocketknife.

Unless you can draw what you wish to accomplish with your bonsai, you're working in the dark. The vision is everything. If you know where you're starting, where you want to go, what the finished tree looks like, your problems, questions, and obstacles seem to melt away. Though bonsai, as living trees, are never truly finished.

4–13

DISPLAY

Good design can be marred by improper display. Let's consider aspects of display that can accentuate the finer qualities of bonsai.

Stands

Like a good bonsai pot, the stand should reflect and complement the tree. Fancy carved and brightly decorated stands go well with opulent Chinese pots and *p'en j'ing*. Most bonsai look best on an understated dark wood stand with simple lines. Sometimes a dull finish is best, but for brightly glazed pots, a shiny, glossy black lacquer is best. The stand should be large enough so that the sides of the pot are not close to the edges of the stand. Nor should the stand be so large that it overwhelms the bonsai. Measure the widest part of the pot from the front. The stand should be at least one and a quarter times that length, but not as long as double that length. In other words, a 10-inch pot should sit on a stand between 12 and 19 inches.

Keep in mind that the tree has an invisible spot in it halfway between the root buttress and the apex. This should be at eye level for the grower and viewer alike. The stand you use can compensate for a display bench that's too high or too low. Historically, miniature bonsai have been placed on a series of high platforms for this very reason.

Figurines

These so-called mud figures are clay sculptures made in the image of bridges, boats, old Chinese men, and more. Historically, the northern Chinese school of *p'en j'ing* and *p'en t'sai* used these figures to attain greater realism and detail in their plantings. Records of their use date back 1,000 years. However, the Japanese, within their cultural heritage, strived to simplify artistic statements in their culinary art, gardens, ikebana, haiku, and, of course, bonsai. The Japanese rejected figurines as unnecessary trappings. But why should I, for instance, as a Swedish–American, reject the complex and diverse *p'en j'ing* Chinese history simply because the Japanese do. Many bonsai growers reject these figurines. But they allow a grower to exercise artistic freedom. I hope that those who use them will be cognizant of their long and rich place in *p'en j'ing* history.

A badly placed figurine can look worse than a poorly placed rock or a gaudy pot. Pay attention to scale.

Three Chinese philosophers, like the figurines in **4–14**, would be having a discussion under an angular old historical tree of some importance. Select a rather tall, hollowed-out fruiting and flowering tree for best results. Nestle these philosophers on a nice, clear green patch of moss to protect them from the noonday sun. After all, they're not playing *ma jong* here at night. Look at the close-up photo **4–15** to see the fine detail in **4–14**.

4–14

4–15

A rocky *p'en j'ing* rising out of the inland sea would not be complete without a Chinese junk (**4–16**). Place this boat so that it is just rounding the back side of a major cliff. If the craft is partially hidden, you can achieve a greater feeling of depth and movement. Remember scale and context when employing these devices. It's better not to use them at all than to use them improperly.

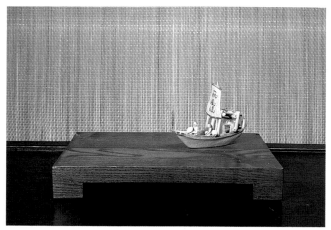

4–16

enjoy the miniatures as accompaniment plantings with this main display.

Garden Display

At the entrance to the Japanese garden, you will find a stone or vessel that contains water (**4–17**). Guests traditionally touch the water or get a refreshing drink from the ladle provided. It is a welcoming ritual found in many societies today, even as an act of religious significance. What a nice way to welcome the visitor to the garden. The sound of running water pouring into itself and the visual display of moisture, ferns, and an inviting drink of cool refreshment.

The *Tokonoma*

In traditional Japanese culture, a display shelf called the *tokonoma* is employed. This large display area covers one wall of a room, usually the front room or area where guests are entertained. A very low shelf holds the shoes or slippers of those invited. A lateral wardrobe may contain garments appropriate to the occasion. Built-in lighting and sliding panels reveal a wonderful stage upon which the master of the house can display his favorite bonsai, calligraphy, paintings, scrolls, viewing stones, figurines, pottery, and more. The composition of this stage is well thought out. Plants, like pine, wish the guest long life, cherry wishes good luck, and so forth. For every major display, such as bonsai, comes an array of accompaniment plantings, such as miniature bonsai, viewing stones (*suiseki*), or dry landscapes (*bonkei*). On the back wall may hang the work of a famous poet or a watercolor rendered by the master's wife. The total composition is impressive indeed, and the message given to the guest is meaningful, complex, profound, yet understated.

Generally, the size of bonsai displayed depends on the size of the room. This makes sense. You would not display a 6-foot-high bonsai in a small dining area, nor would you expect to impress your guests with a 2-inch bonsai on the fireplace mantel. A good rule of thumb is to display 2 inches of bonsai for every 20 square feet in the room. Thus, if your dining area is 8 × 10 feet, its 80 square feet would accommodate an 8-inch-tall bonsai quite nicely. Smaller rooms suit miniature bonsai well, but remember that they can be used in great combinations. This same dining area would enjoy three 4-inch bonsai just as well. A larger room would need a more massive bonsai as its main focal point, but it would

4–17

Bonsai in the garden itself have a complex display problem. A fixed bonsai growing bench is efficient and practical, but for much of the year they won't get the sun conditions they need for optimum performance. Try a portable stand. My trees can be moved about according to the seasons, yet they're still held high for display (**4–18**). The horizontal surface is simply a hardwood stand. The vertical post is painted galvanized pipe.

Style is a combination of personal and cultural input expressed as design. Since the art of bonsai has its roots firmly entrenched in Oriental societies, we are blessed by this rich mix of ancient heritage and individual statement. It is best that beginners copy established styles. Later, as confidence permits, you can discard these "rules," as you wish. Consistency, asymmetry, and interest are three of the most important aspects when developing the design of a bonsai. Five basic styles form the framework to which all styles conform. A bonsai is never finished. Be patient and you can grow to appreciate the refinements only time can grant. Train your trees with an eye for the future. Display them with great care and sensitivity to their potential. Most of all, appreciate the bonsai for what it represents, a link to nature. Become a part of it and it will become a part of you.

4–18

5

MINIATURE
BONSAI
EXAMPLES

5–1

Myrtle, *Myrciaria cauliflora* **(5–1)**
This *komono* bonsai is native to Brazil. Keep this tree
indoors year-round for best results. The container is a
gray, blue, and ivory glazed pot.

5-2

Chinese Snow Rose, *Serrisa foetida* **(5–2)**
This *komono* bonsai is native to southern China, where
it has the common name "tree of a thousand stars." This
tree enjoys being outdoors in full shade during warm
summer months, but it does not tolerate cold. In the
winter, this plant becomes an indoor bonsai. Its blue
black container is Japanese.

5–3

Ming Aralia, *Polyscias fruticosa* (5–3)
This popular indoor plant is a native to tropical Asia.
The leaves are compound and quite elegant, resem-
bling a ribbon-leaved Japanese maple. The blue and
brown dull glazed container was made in the United
States.

5–4

5–6

Sweet Alyssum or Pink Heather, *Lobularia maritima* **(5–4)**

This *keshitsubu* bonsai is one year old, planted from seed. The ¾-inch blue glazed pot is Japanese.

Marigold, *Tagetes erecta* **(5–6)**

This *keshitsubu* bonsai is considerably more dwarfed than its relatives planted in the ground. This plant started out as a 6-inch specimen with fully ruffled double blooms. As the roots became congested, the flower stalks reduced to 1 inch tall and the flower petals reverted to a single conformation.

5–5

5–7

Lobelia or Sapphire, *Lobelia erinus* **(5–5)**

This extremely small *keshitsubu* bonsai is the smallest in my collection. The container is the cap taken from the top of an acorn of white oak.

Chinese Elm or Seiju, *Ulmus parvifolia* **(5–7)**

This *shito* bonsai was grown from a cutting from a larger bonsai. Sometimes in the spring, I plant my trimmings just to see if they will sprout roots. This small tree is 3 years old. The glazed green pot is Japanese.

5—8

5—10

Rhododendron, *Rhododendron pioneer* **(5—8)**
This *katade-mochi* bonsai is deciduous in very cold winters. After a cold snap, the blossoms open before the new leaf buds, giving this spectacular show. The oval cream container is Japanese.

Rhododendron, *Rhododendron impeditum* **(5—10)**
This *shito* bonsai was propagated by earth layering, the favored asexual method for this species. It is two years old, and already it has set blooms for next spring. I can hardly wait! The round blue pot is Japanese.

5—9

5—11

Maidenhair Tree, *Ginkgo biloba* **(5—9)**
This *shito* bonsai will grow up into a *mame* bonsai in two more years. For now, I just find it horticulturally satisfying to keep this hard-to-grow historical species alive in a container this small. The carved black container is Japanese.

Red maple, *Acer rubrum* **(5—11)**
This small group planting is only 9 inches high. The individual trees would be considered *komono* or *mame* bonsai. The completed grove is still a one-handed planting, or *katade-mochi uye*. The flat oval blue tray is Japanese.

5–12

Japanese White Birch, *Betula platyphylla japonica* **(5–12)**
This tree is a classic example of *shohin* bonsai. Notice how it fits comfortably in the palm of the hand. This tree is four years old from seed. The hand-decorated blue and white Japanese container is a signed piece.

5–13

Maidenhair Tree, *Ginkgo biloba* **(5–13)**
Even though the completed grove is a two-handed bonsai, the individual trees range from *katade-mochi* at the tallest to *shito* bonsai at the smallest. The brown oval mica container is Korean.

5–14

Here's the same grove, one year later, in fall color (**5–14**). I find it interesting to compare branch structure from year to year. This is a slow-growing species, especially for development of secondary ramification and interior detail.

5–15

Scotch Pine, *Pinus sylvestris* **(5–15)**
This *katade-mochi* bonsai is coming along quite nicely, considering its young age at fifteen years. The rectangular brown container is Japanese.

Mugo Pine, *Pinus mugo mugo* (5–16)
This *komono* bonsai was originally a demonstration
planting I did for a beginning bonsai class. The bonsai
is doing well and developing nicely. It is ten years old
and planted in a brown rectangular Japanese pot.

5–17

Japanese White Birch, *Betula platyphylla japonica* **(5–17)**
These tiny *shohin* bonsai are only three years old from seed. There are approximately 50 trees in this one-handed grove, or *katade-mochi uye*. The narrow-lipped blue oval container is Japanese.

5–18

Mountain Hemlock, *Tsuga mertensiana* (5–18)
This *katade-mochi* bonsai is a collected specimen from
the 4,000-foot elevation of the Oregon Cascade Mountain range. It is approximately 65 years old and recently designed into this *bunjin* style. The *bunjin* mica
container is Korean.

5–19

Vine Maple, *Acer circinatum* **(5–19)**
This *katade-mochi* bonsai is showing its fall color. This is
a collected specimen, probably 300 years old. The oval
green container is Japanese.

5—20

Red Maple, *Acer rubrum* (5—20)
This grove in its red spring color is shown in **5—11**. In the fall, yellow autumn colors will show. In cold, dry winters, this grove will turn from yellow back to a brilliant red again before the leaves fall. In a wet fall, the colors would be green and yellow before the trunks show bare twigs.

6

TRAINING
TECHNIQUES

PRINCIPLES OF GROWTH

Basic Outline

When we observe healthy trees in their natural environment, one of the first things we notice is their outline. A cluster of stately oaks intertwine their branches, each tree having a well-rounded outline, almost ball-shaped. Pine trees are usually taller than they are wide with a slightly rounded apex. Prostrate junipers tend to hug close to the ground following the contours of adjacent rocks and crevices. A tall row of poplar trees or untrimmed Italian cypress form a tall, pointed shape straight up to the sky.

These basic outlines reflect the hormones inherent to the species. A tall plant has great concentrations of growth hormone at its apex. Also, its outline shape indicates that just the reverse is true along its side and bottom branches. Just the opposite is found in trees that are wider than they are tall. On these wide trees, growth hormone is concentrated toward the sides rather than the top of the tree.

The bonsai grower may take advantage of this natural phenomenon rather than fight it. Choose a general shape for the bonsai consistent with the full-size species. For example, a bonsai arborvitae would be easy to train into the formal upright style due to its strong tendency to grow a straight, upright trunk. Conversely, it would be a struggle to try to form a weeping or cascading style of arborvitae. Maples, which are generally about as wide as they are tall, make good candidates for the broom style or informal upright style. A prostrate juniper makes a difficult upright style, but quite naturally forms the windswept, semicascade, or cascade styles.

Trimming Techniques

Each species of plant grows in a slightly different way. It should not be surprising to learn that each species has an indicated method of trimming as well. Obviously, it would be impossible to list the thousands of bonsai-appropriate species here and to describe the pruning method that works best. But let's consider some of the most common trees.

Pine

New needles on a pine tree extend themselves in spring in a tight cluster known as a "candle." This upright succulent growth on a vigorously growing tree can be removed in its entirety just as it starts to show individual needles. About a month later, new candles will form and open up. Choose among these secondary candles the ones useful for your design, removing the strong vertical buds as they appear. On mature or slow-growing pine, it is preferable to retain a portion of the primary candles which first appear in spring. On these trees, remove most of the length of the medium candles and retain the entire length of the smallest candles. This will help even out the growth. On weak or unhealthy trees, candle removal is inappropriate.

Maple

These trees grow branches that continually push out new growth from spring to early summer (**6–1**). Some early fall growth is normally seen as well. A new branch will have pairs of leaves along its length. These pairs will be aligned both horizontally and vertically; so, careful observation is necessary. If two opposite leaves are aligned in a horizontal fashion—side to side—the next pair will emerge vertically, or one up and one down. This pattern is very regular and predictable. To prune, choose one horizontal pair, and wait until two

6–1

more pairs of leaves emerge beyond them. Then cut off those two pairs of leaves. You don't need to make the cut close to the leaves; halfway between the first and second pair is sufficient. New growth will emerge in a nice horizontal fashion at the bases of the first pair of leaves. Now, instead of one twig, you have formed two. Repeat the above pruning to turn two twigs into four twigs, and so on. You will be forming a wonderful branch network that will contribute to the illusion of age.

Elm

These trees have branches where the leaves appear at regular alternating intervals. Simply choose the direction that you want new growth to go. Leaves will appear in a pattern of up, down, right side, left side, up, down, and so on. If you desire growth to go down, for example, simply choose a leaf facing down and prune halfway between that leaf and the next one. For best results, let the new growth extend beyond this desired leaf at least two more leaves before pruning.

Juniper

These conifers are constant growers from early spring through late fall. Once the branch has been placed in its proper style position, maintenance trimming is easy. Simply rub out unwanted buds as they form. Growth that extends itself into unwanted areas, such as straight up or straight down, can be removed, using your fingertips with a gentle pull (**6–2**). The new growth will separate easily when tender and young. If you neglect your juniper bonsai for two weeks or more, you will have to use pruning shears because the new growth will have hardened off.

A juniper displays its immature, rapidly growing foliage in **6–3**. This typical growth is sharp to the touch and should be discouraged on bonsai specimens. In the center of the photo, this juniper has converted one of its shoots into the more desirable mature form of growth. This secondary growth is a softer needle-type of foliage that compacts well for bonsai purposes. Heavy pruning with trimming shears will cause this desirable old growth to revert to the faster-growing immature form. To maintain the older growth, pinch it back lightly with your fingertips, using a gentle pulling action. The needle-type growth will easily separate at its growth junctions and will stimulate it to divide and redivide into a nice compact cushion of green foliage.

6–3

Fir, Larch, Spruce, Hemlock

These conifers grow from adventitious buds along the branch. To activate these buds, remove the young terminal tip with thumb and forefinger. Once these secondary buds start to extend themselves, keep them compact by removing half their length while they're still young and succulent. Several growth spurts occur with these species; so, be attentive to your trees from spring until late summer. Remove unwanted growth as soon as it appears. Shorten wanted growth before it becomes attenuated and leggy.

Flowering Trees

All flowering trees that do not bear fruit can be easily pruned. Wait for the flowers to fade, then prune back heavily. You will have to accomplish one year's worth of

6–2

pruning at this time; so, be aggressive. One month later, a number of suckers or water sprouts will appear. Trim these off as desired. Sometimes a short length of this growth can be kept compact by removing most of its length. This once-a-year pruning method guarantees that the tree will bloom the following year, regardless of the time of bloom.

Trees Producing Flowers and Fruit

For trees that produce both flowers and fruit (**6–4**), the correct pruning technique is slightly more complex. Obviously the method for flowering trees will not work because heavy pruning right after flowering (**6–5**) will also trim away the fruit. For these trees, wait until the fruit drops off. Then trim only half of the branches. So, if your tree has thirty branches, prune back heavily on fifteen. Space this pruning around your tree to maintain its general shape and style. The following year trim back the other fifteen branches. This way, you will always have a tree with both one- and two-year-old branches on it. In other words, it will always be both fruiting and flowering (**6–6**).

6–5

6–6

6–4

Trees with Compound Leaves

For trees with compound leaves, such as pistachio, mountain ash, walnut, and clematis, pruning must attend to the new leaf bud. In a compound leaf, the long, branch-like structure that holds all the leaves isn't really a branch. An attempt to prune this "branch" will not achieve anything. All you're actually doing is trimming away part of the leaf. The leaf itself is a combination of ten or more leaflets that make up a single true leaf. To prune this tree, realize that the new bud appears at the base of the compound leaf only. Then just prune the tree as if it were an elm.

ROOT GROWTH AND ROOT PRUNING

When we think of roots, we tend to imagine a tangled bunch of stiff and inflexible woody fibers that keep the tree from falling down. Since this aspect of root structure is the most predominant, we assume it to be the most important. Actually, in bonsai, roots have only two functions, and neither offers real physical support for the tree. Surface roots give the *appearance of age* to a bonsai, and their presence on the soil surface gives *visual stability to the design*. Without the trunk flaring out sideways just above the soil surface, the bonsai looks as though it is a recent cutting just stuck into the ground.

Underneath the soil surface, these large roots divide instantly into a mass of tiny root hairs. These white root tips are actually the only functional aspect of the root mass for bonsai purposes. Once the young and succulent root tip hardens into a brown root, it no longer is part of this functional relationship with the plant. All the root does when it is brown and tough is use up space in the pot, contributing to the condition of being pot-bound. A bonsai can rely on these crowded roots to help dwarf the foliage, but you need to keep this effect in control at all times or it could be fatal for the tree.

I like to consider the state of being pot-bound in terms of volume percentage. A totally pot-bound tree has no soil remaining in the root ball. Inside the container are only roots, no soil. In volume, this can be expressed as 100 percent roots and 0 percent soil, or 100 percent pot-bound. A bonsai that is 50 percent root-bound, therefore, has half roots and half soil in its container. In this condition, some dwarfing forces are imparted by the roots toward the foliage. At 60 percent root-bound these forces become stronger, but at 100 percent root-bound, the dwarfing forces are so strong that they kill the plant.

Growing bonsai in a small container requires a balance between the strong visual roots, the tender white root tips, and the congested root mass which dwarfs the tree. If a plant gets to be 90 percent root-bound, it is very difficult to repot because the roots are so congested that they're nearly impossible to untangle and trim. A 60 percent root-bound plant is easy to repot because the soil content is still high enough that the roots can easily be separated and trimmed. So, a good rule is never to allow your bonsai to exceed 85 percent root-bound at any time, and to only transplant them into a condition of at least 50 percent root-bound. By adhering to this range of being pot-bound, the grower not only continues to control foliage growth but ensures successful trimming of the root ball, too. In sum, the bonsai grower always inspects the roots from time to time, repotting before the soil content falls below 15 percent by volume in the container. Then, during root pruning, never remove so many roots that the soil content in the new container rises above 50 percent.

The golden threadbranch cypress, *Chamaecyparis pisifera filifera* 'Aurea', shown in **6–7**, has been getting progressively more root-bound. This year, it reached the critical stage with only 15 percent soil remaining in the pot. Close inspection with a root hook (**6–8**) shows what roots look like when they are surrounded by only 15 percent soil. Notice that they can, with some effort, still be separated and untangled. If I had left this bonsai alone for one more year, these roots would not untangle as easily. They would rip apart and be torn in numerous places, and transplanting would have taken

6–7

6–8

much more time and effort. Also, the tree's health would have been at risk. Instead, these roots can be gently combed out. Some longer roots can be trimmed back. The new, smaller root ball can be placed into a slightly larger pot to compensate for the slightly larger tree that has developed over the years (6—9). Make a mental guesstimate after root pruning to get as close to 50 percent roots and 50 percent fresh bonsai soil in this new container. It is important to keep the roots moist at all times during transplant. It is also critical that some, not all, roots be left untrimmed. If all white root tips are trimmed off, you'll endanger the life of the tree. After this bonsai is in its new ceramic home, generously water it for the next ten days. The uncut roots, with their white root tips still intact, will support the plant while the cut roots manufacture new white tips.

6—9

After transplanting, a few clumps of moss may be placed on the soil surface and the edges carefully covered with soil. If the moss is partially buried, it won't dry out and it'll survive the transplant. Clumps of moss just plunked down on the soil surface will dry out, curl up on the edges, and die (**6–10**). Moss should never cover more than two-thirds of the soil surface, or it will begin to interfere with soil drainage and respiration.

Root tips like to grow when they're half in air and half in water. The reason we screen out small particles of soil from our bonsai growing mix is to create room for air inside the pot. When white roots congregate on the outside edge of the root ball, it is because they are gasping for air. The new growing tip finds the soil mix inside the pot too heavy when its particle size is too small. In an effort to gain air, the root escapes this heavy root ball and grows alongside the moist surface of the ceramic pot which breathes air to the roots. Properly screened bonsai soil will make it unnecessary for the roots to have to escape to the sides of the pot.

6–10

BONSAI SOIL

Most bonsai enthusiasts are reluctant to accept that there could be such a thing as bonsai soil. Somehow the concept that orchids grow best in an orchid-growing medium is easier to grasp. That specialized plants such as cactus, venus fly trap, and bird of paradise need specially formulated soils is acceptable. But bonsai soil?

Near the turn of the twentieth century, when bonsai was first being introduced into Europe and America, bonsai failed to thrive, starting a rumor that there was some Oriental secret to growing these plants. That notion has been dispelled and replaced with basic botanical knowledge. One of the main so-called secrets was making bonsai soil.

Advantages of Good Bonsai Soil

- increased oxygen to the roots
- improved drainage
- easier to transplant without damage to root hairs
- roots comb out better for pruning
- greater surface area on which roots can grow
- increase in the number of root branches and frequency of their divisions
- less dangerous heat rise in the pot in hot weather
- correct pH of soil for species
- ideal conditions for ion exchange
- suitable medium for development of healthful bacteria
- excellent color for best display
- easier to apply and control nutrients
- less damage due to root rot
- reduced twig dieback on deciduous trees
- long-term success—trees will be healthier each year

There are five main considerations when making bonsai soil: particle size, texture, soil composition, microorganisms, and aesthetics.

Particle Size

Consider two cubes. I will assign sizes to these cubes to demonstrate a surprising and unexpected principle important to soils, especially potting soils.

Cube A is 1 inch on each edge. Two things can be said about Cube A: its volume (V) is 1 cubic inch and its surface area (S) is 6 square inches. Or simply, $V = 2$ inches and $S = 6$ inches.

Cube B is 2 inches on each edge. Its volume and surface then are, $V = 8$ inches and $S = 24$ inches.

Roots grow on surfaces of soil particles, not just "in" the dirt. Seen through a microscope, the meristematic area, or growing tip, seeks out pockets of readily available water adjacent to air. Residual water clings to surfaces of soil particles and air channels are found passing nearby. Where there's water but not air, and vice versa, there is no meristematic growth.

Which of the cubes makes the best soil particle, A or

B? Cube A has a surface area of 6 square inches, whereas Cube B would provide 24 square inches. Cube B seems better, but Cube B would occupy eight times the volume in the pot as Cube A—not a good tradeoff for having only four times the surface area. This can be expressed:

Cube A			Cube B		
Surface	6	*which is better than*	Surface	24	3
Volume	1		Volume	8	1

A cube half the size of Cube A would have a surface-to-volume ratio of 12, clearly superior to Cube A. This establishes the principle that as soil particles become smaller, they increase surface area rather dramatically without using up much room in the pot. So how small can we make these particles? There's a limit somewhere.

Liquids have an unusual property, surface tension. What does this have to do with bonsai soil? If soil particles are so close together that the surface tension of water creates a capillary effect, the water will rise against gravity or cling to the particles. A bonsai pot filled with such a soil would not allow roots to grow because most of the interstitial spaces would still be occupied by water and not air. Evaporation might briefly dry out the soil. Then the plant would have some oxygen, but it would soon be fighting for water. Roots would perform poorly, and new buds would be small, discolored, and weak. It would be difficult to get the soil wet once it was dry and difficult to get it dry once it was wet. Some roots would rot every winter, and, finally, after about 2½ years, the bonsai dies. Sound familiar?

If soil particles are no smaller than ³⁄₃₂ inch, this scenario can be avoided. Fortunately, this is an easy size to achieve. Just discard any part of the soil that passes through a common window screen.

Getting rid of large, inefficient particles (Cube B) is easy too. Discard any particles that will not pass through ⅛-inch hardware cloth, sometimes called soffit screen. A square frame about 16 × 16 inches and 3 inches deep is all you need. Staple the appropriate screen or hardware cloth to the frame. Bonsai nurseries have inexpensive sifting screens available that will last a lifetime.

A related soil issue concerns the common practice of sprinkling loose gravel, clay pot chips, or stones into the bottom of the pot in order to improve drainage. Even Japanese literature shows the bonsai pot being striated or layered with a coarse soil mix in the bottom of the pot. Recent research in soil science indicates that this may actually do more harm than good. Water tends to move from a large particle toward a smaller particle. So, these pebbles create an upward migration of moisture, resulting in a shortage of water for the deeper roots and a buildup of salts. Many bonsai masters are beginning to agree. The pot that drains best is the one that contains a homogeneous mix from top to bottom, with no change in particle size and no interfaces between soil types.

Texture

Consider two particles—one smooth and one rough that are the same size. The rough particle has a much greater surface area per volume. The rough particle is, therefore, a more efficient soil particle for our bonsai pot.

Imagine two types of particles in separate bins. One is washed river sand, and the other is pumice. Through a microscope the roots of a bonsai maple slide and skid along between the polished surfaces of river sand. In the other bin, seen microscopically, the maple's roots divide and redivide into thousands of tiny root hairs as they are irritated by the miniature, irregular, rugged particles. A remarkable macroscopic result is that the branches are more twiggy, detailed, and twisted. They also exhibit a higher degree of ramification. Root character and development are expressed in the branch structure as well. Therefore, when selecting soil components, favor the rugged to the smooth and the irregular over the polished.

On a hot summer day, residual moisture in irregular, rugged soil particles becomes quite important in maintaining a modest temperature in the bonsai pot. Roots above 90° F (32.2° C) start to go dormant. They stop putting out new growth to protect against dehydration. Any further temperature increase causes damage. These moisture reservoirs in the soil particles act like tiny evaporative coolers and can assist the bonsai in making it through the summer without stress, without twig dieback or the curly brown leaf edges we despise. If you've ever grown a Japanese maple bonsai, you know what I'm referring to.

Soil Composition

Most of us understand that an ideal soil for one plant, such as an azalea, would be unsuitable for a different plant, such as a juniper. Let's look at some of the reasons.

A line graph that includes all the pH conditions under which plants can survive might look something like this.

pH   0 ———————————————— 100
    Acid   **Alkaline**

The numbers 0 and 100 are arbitrary ends of the scale rather than actual pH values. This is a bit theoretical and imprecise, but it helps illustrate related factors. *Satsuki* azalea at 23, butterfly maple at 41, crab apple at 56, and *shimpaku* juniper at 74 all grow in a different soil.

Optimum soil pH for such species is most often the pH found in the native soil. The azalea in nature grows as a small spreading bush found in shady areas under the spreading canopy of taller climax trees. Azalea roots are found in layers of decaying organic matter made up of fallen leaves from itself and surrounding trees. (The word *organic* means "alive at one time," that is, composed of carbon-containing compounds, not to be confused with the absence of pesticides.) The *shimpaku* juniper, by contrast, are themselves climax trees. They grow mostly in pockets of decomposed rock formed by constant freezing and thawing of the ledges over time. What little organic matter the roots grow in has been dropped by the juniper itself over a long period of time in sparse quantities. The high mineral content of the rock contributes to the high alkaline pH of the soil.

For further comparison, consider these graphs.

Leaf Size   0 ——————↓——————↓—————— 100
    Large azalea   juniper **Small**

The azalea is located in the twenties for comparative leaf size, whereas the juniper, because of its small needles, is found in the seventies.

There is a similar correspondence for ultraviolet light tolerance.

UV Light   0 ——————↓——————↓—————— 100
    Intolerant azalea   juniper **Tolerant**

And this scale measuring soil composition reveals the relative proportions of organic and inorganic materials for the azalea and juniper.

Soil Composition
    0 ——————↓——————↓—————— 100
100%   **100%**
Organic azalea   juniper **Inorganic**

The serious bonsai enthusiast has two bins full of soil particles waiting at all times, screened, of course. One of the bins contains 100 percent organic particles, like bark, sawdust, leaf mold, shavings, steer manure, or compost from the garden. The other bin contains 100 percent inorganic particles, like decomposed granite, sharp sand, pumice, vermiculite, perlite, lava cinders, and more. These inorganic particles have never been alive and are high in mineral content and high in alkaline pH.

As an example, suppose you are repotting a Japanese

black pine. What is the soil composition?

pH 0 —————————————— 100
     Acid   **?**   **Alkaline**
You don't know, doesn't seem acid though.

UV Light 0 —————————————— 100
    Intolerant   80%   **Tolerant**
You know it tolerates a lot of sun.

Leaf Size 0 —————————————— 100
    Large   70?   **Small**
Big needles, bigger than juniper anyway.

Using these scales, the approximate soil composition for Japanese black pine would be 75 percent inorganic. This is just about right. Try out these scales on your own; they're useful for all species.

Some major plant species are listed in five groups as examples to help guide you to correct soil mixing. This plant list is necessarily incomplete. Getting the composition exactly right is not critical because particle size is more important than pH.

Group 1 *Three-fourths organic, one-fourth inorganic*
Azalea, rhododendron, bald cypress, redwood, tropical foliage plants

Group 2 *Two-thirds organic, one-third inorganic*
Alder, birch, beech, hornbeam, elm, zelkova, dogwood, maple

Group 3 *One-half organic, one-half inorganic*
Pyracantha, wisteria, quince, fig, corokia, holly, boxwood, apple, peach, pear, cherry, plum, cotoneaster

Group 4 *One-third organic, two-thirds inorganic*
Larch, ginkgo, fir, spruce, hemlock, cypress, cryptomeria

Group 5 *One-fourth organic, three-fourths inorganic*
Oak, pine, juniper, jade, eucalyptus, alpine and desert plants

Microorganisms

Fertile soil is never sterile. The word *sterile*, though, is sometimes used commercially to indicate a product that's weed-free. A bag of potting soil will often tout the word *sterile* as a reassurance that the bag contains good stuff, not bad stuff. If the soil were really sterile, it would house no bacteria, no spores, no seeds, no molds, no fungi, no viruses, no insects, no eggs, no larvae, etc. When the potting soil container says the soil is sterile, that suggests it contains no insects and no disease.

Many plants take advantage of microorganisms to aid their life processes. *Fertile soil* is full of microorganisms. Many forms of bacteria contribute to the breakdown of soil. The effects are quite beneficial and contribute to *ion exchange*. Excellent ion exchange indicates a lack of important chemical interactions, resulting in reduced nutrient exchange, limited moisture uptake, and, in general, a slowing down of the biochemistry that supports the life of the plant.

Soil Components to Avoid

Any soil without weeds growing in it.

Roadside soil It may contain asphalt residues, pesticides, and dust that's difficult to wash out. There will be no beneficial bacteria.

Beach sand or soils They contain salt and other minerals, and trying to wash them out is usually inefficient and incomplete.

River sand The edges of particles have been polished smooth over time. There are no beneficial cracks and crevices for roots, moisture, nutrients, or helpful bacteria.

Manures as soil They may contain straw and undigested organic material, but the remaining time these materials will stay firm and particulate is limited. They will break down completely and result in soil compaction. A manure slurry fertilizer, however, is beneficial, and manure as a soil *amendment* is fine.

High-mineral soils Beware because these have often been formed as a result of sedimentation of alkali or brackish lakebeds in high desert areas.

Discarded soil It is tempting to reuse potting soil, but I cannot recommend it. Why didn't the former plant thrive? What was the former plant treated with in its lifetime? Perhaps nothing, but insecticides, fungicides, and nonutilized fertilizers may be present. It's best to start anew.

Used kitty litter Even though you screen out the solid waste, the urine does not wash out easily or completely.

Deodorized kitty litter The little blue or green particles in this type of kitty litter contain dyes and fragrances that affect soil performance in a negative way.

Aquarium gravel These gravels are highly polished, which is bad, or artificially colored, which is worse. They may be coated with a substance to make them attractive under black lights.

Fine peat moss These materials are nitrogen-starved. They will rob nitrogen from the plant faster than you can fertilize it. When the nitrogen finally reaches a level high enough for the material, it's too high for the plant. Scum forms on the surface of the soil, blocking air and interfering with watering and drainage. Use only dark, well-rotted, and stabilized wood products. I prefer hemlock bark for its lack of slivers.

Perhaps the most interesting microorganisms in bonsai soil, or any soil, are fungi that attach themselves to roots in the form of nodules quite visible to the naked eye. This symbiotic association of the mycelium of a fungus with the roots of a seed plant is called *mycorrhiza*. The fungus derives water and nutrients from the root, thereby eliminating the necessity for leaves. The plant benefits from the nodule because the fungus can process atmospheric nitrogen as a nutrient. Your bonsai can benefit from this relationship if you inoculate your bonsai soil with a known population of fungus.

When transplanting bonsai, I usually retain a bit of the old soil and transfer it along with the tree. When collecting trees from the woods, make sure you bring some well-rotted organic material along with the tree. Find an established, mature tree of the same species and brush off the top layer of recently fallen needles. Look for a slightly moist, partly rotted layer of needles below. This layer appears slightly frosted with beneficial molds and fungi and has a characteristic rich, woodsy smell similar to Camembert rind. Dig up a couple of handfuls, making sure to include the top layer of soil as well. Keep this soil moist in a plastic container until you're ready to plant your tree; then make a slurry or suspension of your moldy needles by stirring them briskly in a bucket of water. Pour the container of water over the root area of your newly transplanted specimen. This technique benefits trees planted in the ground as well as trees planted in a container. You can apply this technique to all species, not just pine.

Aesthetics

I like to think of bonsai as half-horticulture and half-art. That way of thinking serves me well when I want to stress the importance of a soil's color. From a purely

horticultural standpoint, the tree doesn't care about the color of the soil from which it is growing. I must admit, however, my personal dissatisfaction with white-colored particles in some bonsai soils. There is something unsettling, rather cluttered, and messy about seeing perlite in bonsai soil. I find some pumices to be better, but still quite obvious after a summer rain. Even vermiculite has rather crystalline flecks in its makeup, and, to my artistic sense, red lava cinders have a distracting hue. Over time I have come to appreciate black lava cinders and decomposed dark rock as two superior inorganic soil components. They hold their color well, yet exhibit a wet-dry color change obvious enough to assist in setting watering schedules.

My favorite organic particle is hemlock bark. After having been aged for a year in the presence of steer and chicken manure, it turns a dark, rich brown, almost black color. It holds its particle size for about 5 years, making it one of the best organic materials around for older potted specimens that enjoy frequent repotting.

With all soils, the final test of a good soil is its performance with plant material. Try to grow radishes in your prospective bonsai soil mix. Set up small experiments adding vitamin B_1 to one and not another, or plant seeds in your organic or inorganic mix alone and in various proportions. These experiments help take the guesswork out of your bonsai soil. Observe the radish plants carefully. A plant that starts out with a flourish only to yellow, weaken, and become nonproductive will guide you to what you need to add to your soil to keep your bonsai happy. A lush radish tip, but no vegetable root, tells you that the soil lacks phosphorus and potassium. You need to nurture bonsai growing in this medium with 0–10–10 each winter. Look for chlorotic leaves which tell you that iron, sulfur, nitrogen, or trace minerals are lacking. Keep trying to grow that perfect radish. In the end, your persistence and unbiased observation will lead you to the bonsai soil that works best for you, taking into consideration your individual watering habits, your personal schedule, the plant's requirements, and, of course, the climate.

7

CREATING
MINIATURE
BONSAI

PROPAGATION

From Seed

Most bonsai seed (**7–1**) can be classified as either hardy or not. For most high-altitude conifers, Japanese maple, and high-desert species, the seed is considered hardy. Therefore, the seed requires a period of cold stratification before germination is possible. I have found the following technique useful for these plants hard to grow from seed (**7–2**).

Three months before spring, drop the seed into a large vessel containing standing water heated to 100° F (45° C). Do not reheat the water. Soak the seed in this pot for the next two days, gently stirring it once in a while. Allow the water and the seed to gradually cool to room temperature. Remove the seed and blot out excess moisture with a damp towel. Do not dry com-

7–2

pletely. Treat the seed with a fungicide, such as Captan, and place it in a plastic bag with moist humus or sphagnum moss. Do not seal the bag, but allow one end to remain slightly open, and place the bag in the coldest part of your refrigerator. If the mixture of humus and seed accidentally freezes, it is still fine, but it's not necessary to freeze it. From time to time, check the contents of the bag. The moss and seed mix should be moist at all times, neither dry nor visibly wet.

Plant this seed outside after the oak trees leaf out in your area, usually in late spring. This will ensure that the ground is warm enough to stimulate germination. Seed that sits in cold earth usually sulks and then rots. Plant in a light, loose soil that drains extremely well. Cover the seed with soil no more than two diameters of the seed itself. Keep the soil moist, not soggy, and be sure to protect the area from birds and rodents. Fertilize lightly when the seedlings are 1 inch high. Thin and transplant taller seedlings as soon as it's safe; their roots should be about 3 inches long. Some seed will require two years to germinate. Do not discard the seed unless it's visibly rotted.

In colder climates it may be sufficient to allow Mother Nature to do the cold stratification. Place the seed in a planting tray or seed box with well-draining soil. Cover it with wire screen and place it on the ground in your garden. Protect the box with a loose layer of fallen leaves or snow, and keep your fingers crossed. In spring you may have a healthy crop of fine, hardy seedlings.

For nonhardy seed, such as annuals, perennials,

7–1

grasses, warm-climate trees, and the like, sow the seed in a planting box in late spring. Water lightly and often; then follow the above suggestions for transplanting and fertilizing.

Air Layering

This method of propagation is extremely useful for bonsai, especially miniature bonsai, and it's recommended even for beginners. The success rate is fairly high (about 80 percent) if you closely adhere to the following suggestions. Locate a branch that has visual interest. Try to imagine a bonsai above where you attempt to make roots grow. Locate an area with trunk movement, tapering, and a variety of side branches for a compact bonsai. Wrap a sheet of clear plastic around the potential bonsai. At the bottom of this bag, secure the plastic tightly with a loop of copper wire right where you want new roots to grow. With a pair of pliers, tighten the wire as snugly as you can, preferably so that the wire actually starts to damage the trunk. Place extremely moist, soaked sphagnum moss over the wire, pull down the plastic over the top of the moss, and secure it lightly at the bottom with string or floral tape. You've created a bag that will totally enclose the future root area below the wire. There should be a generous amount of moss enclosed within this newly formed plastic sleeve. The moss should extend from slightly above the wire to several inches below. Now cover this bag with another layer of plastic, this time, black plastic. This wrapping will help to heat the future root area as well as protect the developing root mass from harmful light and ultraviolet rays.

On slow-growing species, new roots will form within a year. Faster-growing plants, like elm or maple, will form roots within a few months. The advantage of the black plastic layer will become evident as you raise it to check for new roots. You won't be disturbing the growing area. If roots do not appear quickly, it may be necessary to add additional moisture to the moss from time to time. I just squirt water inside with a syringe.

Root Layering

It always amazes me to see how nature will propagate its species without help from gardeners. The process of root layering seems, at first glance, to be a rather artificial way of producing a new plant, but some species naturally depend on it. A low-lying branch of juniper resting on the ground will sprout new roots easily. A low rhododendron branch or azalea branch will do the

same. I have seen hard-to-propagate species, like high-altitude conifers, root their lower branches when covered with soil. Nursery stock, such as little gem spruce, andelyensis cypress, and boxwood, will develop roots on the lower branches if they've been planted a little too low in their containers. The lower branches shown in **7–3** and **7–4** are all rooted.

7–3

7–4

The technique for producing your own root layering is quite easy. Cut away some bark from a low-lying tree branch, and bend the branch down so that the freshly cut area is covered with soil. Rub the freshly cut surface with rooting hormone. This simple method of propagation has the distinct advantage that if your roots don't form, the branch remains alive. So, you can try again. This isn't true with a cutting or a slip from a plant; unsuccessful cuttings die. Failed root layerings, however, live on for another treatment.

Cuttings

A wide variety of plant material is suitable for miniature bonsai. Not all these plants will be easy to propagate by cuttings. In general, if the plant grows quickly, it is a possible candidate for this technique. Commercial growers use special heated cutting beds, automatic misting systems, and specialized hormone formulas. This enables them to propagate even the toughest slow-growing conifer by cuttings. For the average home gardener, these techniques are impractical. Here's a simple method of taking cuttings that works well for me. Try it and if the plant still doesn't sprout roots, it may be just too difficult a species.

Prepare in advance a cutting box or medium seed pot. Smaller containers dry out too rapidly. Fill it with coarse sand or perlite and water well. Cuttings should be taken in late spring or early summer for best results. Collect small branches from the host plant and immediately immerse them in a pan of water. Place them in a refrigerator storage container that has a sealing type of lid. Move the entire project indoors out of the sun.

In a small shallow cup, mix an appropriate amount of liquid rooting hormone according to the directions on the label. Select a small branch from the water vessel, cut off a small section of the branch about 4 inches long, and trim off about half of the foliage with a sharp pair of pruning shears. Place the cut end of the 4-inch cutting in the cup of hormone, and turn it into a 3-inch cutting by cutting it again *under water*. For best results, cut at a diagonal across a visible bud or node. With the new cut still in the hormone, count slowly to ten while making a preparatory hole in the sand mix with a sharp end of your pruning tool.

Transfer the cutting without hesitation to the cutting box and immediately push sand around the stem. There should be about half of the cutting above the medium and half buried below. A slightly slanting cutting will root better than a vertical one. After you are through taking cuttings, apply a heavy mist of lukewarm water to the foliage, and cover the foliage with a transparent plastic cover or polyvinyl sheeting. Place the box where it can get some light and room-temperature heat. A window box facing east is ideal. Keep the box out of the sun's direct rays. Mist as often as you can, several times a day minimum. Check cautiously for roots after three weeks, but do not despair if there are none yet. A green cutting might still sprout roots. Discard the obviously withered ones as you see them so that you do not allow dead cuttings to contaminate your box with rot. Transfer the rooted cuttings to larger individual containers when the new roots are 2 inches long.

Grafting

One grafting technique is appropriate for miniature bonsai. Most grafts are too large and bulky for these tiny plants. A side graft is too obvious, a root graft impractical, an end graft usually ruins the trunk taper, and a Phoenix graft is inappropriate for smaller specimens. The *thread graft*, however, is valuable for growing bonsai miniatures. In the workshop section which follows, notice that the miniature bonsai grower selects plant material that's not only thick-trunked and compact, but it must also have lower branches that can serve as a future apex after severe pruning. In some cases, a plant has tremendous potential due to its superior trunk taper, root buttress, and small foliage size, but its foliage is just not low enough on the trunk. This is an excellent opportunity to use the thread graft.

Take a long, supple branch from high on the tree and strip off all the leaves. This will leave you with a long live whip in an artificial deciduous condition. Measure the size of the woody stem carefully, and find a drill bit that's slightly larger in diameter. Drill a hole clear through the trunk at the level that you desire branches, and thread the whip through the hole. Do not cut off this branch, just bend it in a downward loop. Secure the whip in the hole on the far side by driving a straight pin through the branch at the exact place where it brushes against the cambium of the trunk. In maples, this graft will take hold in a few months. On slow-growing pine, it will take two years, but this technique is almost always successful. After the graft has joined, remove the downward loop and you'll have a nice tiny lower branch on your previously bare trunk.

Let's create miniature bonsai from common plants we can find in nurseries, our own gardens (that we've propagated), and from the wild.

Creating Miniature Bonsai from Larger Bonsai

The *chumono* bonsai rhododendron (*Rhododendron impeditum*) in **7–5** is fairly mediocre. The trunk is interesting but not very large and the quasibroom style branches quite ordinary. Let's convert this bonsai into a miniature bonsai, thereby making the trunk look thicker and eliminating the shrubby structure of the branches.

Notice the trunk from this side (**7–6**). It almost appears to be formed by the union of two plants. The surface rootage is mostly absent except for one strong root on the right side. Let's look at the other side for comparison.

From this side (**7–7**), the trunk is unified from top to bottom. The surface roots are a bit larger and well distributed, which gives the bonsai a feeling of strength and stability. The branch structure from this side is cluttered and random, which is why the other side was chosen as the front of the large bonsai. For a miniature bonsai, this front is better because most of the branches will be removed.

Start removing some of these unwanted branches to define a specific trunk line (**7–8**). The largest branch on the left seems to be the best candidate for a new

7–5

7–7

7–6

7–8

7–9

7–11

7–10

7–12

7–13

Notice the trunk from this side (**7–6**). It almost appears to be formed by the union of two plants. The surface rootage is mostly absent except for one strong root on the right side. Let's look at the other side for comparison.

From this side (**7–7**), the trunk is unified from top to bottom. The surface roots are a bit larger and well distributed, which gives the bonsai a feeling of strength and stability. The branch structure from this side is cluttered and random, which is why the other side was chosen as the front of the large bonsai. For a miniature bonsai, this front is better because most of the branches will be removed.

Start removing some of these unwanted branches to define a specific trunk line (**7–8**). The largest branch on the left seems to be the best candidate for a new

7–5

7–7

7–6

7–8

7–9

7–11

7–10

7–12

7–13

trunk. Unfortunately, there are no small branches along its lower length; so, we'll have to cut it back severely and wait for new buds to form.

By cutting off the end of the trunk here, we can take advantage of the nice, natural bends in the trunk (**7–9**). This will add more visual interest to the finished planting. New buds will begin to form in about two weeks.

With the remaining branches so numerous (**7–10**), we can select those that are best for our miniature bonsai and trim away branches that are crowded, redundant, or that clutter the style. To the right is a potential pot candidate for the newly styled miniature. Its round shape will blend nicely with the rounded curves of the plant's trunk and branches.

With most of the branches removed (**7–11**), we can now safely transplant this rhododendron into the smaller container. The tools shown are some of my favorites for repotting—a small red-handled root hook, tweezers with a potting chisel, a root rake with double-edged potting trowel, chopsticks, and a large root hook shown in my hand. Keep the roots moist at all times with a spray bottle of water.

Test the new, smaller root ball in the miniature container (**7–12**). Allow sufficient wiggle room around the roots so that you can incorporate fresh bonsai soil. Pack the new soil in and around the roots with a gentle thrusting motion with the chopsticks. Position the tree trunk so that it does not look as though it's falling forward or backwards. A gentle side-to-side angle is often pleasant.

The plant in **7–13** is positioned correctly in its new pot. When viewed from the side, the apex is directly above the trunk line. From the front, the surface roots show slightly, and the trunk tapers dramatically from the large root buttress up to the narrow top.

A few weeks later, an astonishing number of new buds start to become visible (**7–14**). Select the best buds now and remove unwanted buds carefully with a pair of tweezers. There's no point encouraging growth to extend into undesirable locations on the plant. Notice that even the stringy-looking branches are getting a nice crop of secondary buds. Rub or pinch out secondary buds that want to grow straight up or straight down. Retain and encourage new horizontal shoots.

Remove unwanted buds along the trunk line as soon as they form (**7–15**). If you wait, the plant's strength will go into forming an unwanted branch. Then you'll have to remove this superfluous growth later with a concave cutter, and it will contribute to additional scarring of the trunk line.

7–14

7–15

7–16

Moss may be added to the soil surface at this time (**7–16**). Not only does it make the bonsai look more finished, but it helps retain moisture for this moisture-loving bonsai. Be sure not to cover more than half of the soil surface. Arrange the moss so that it looks natural. For the best appearance, use irregularly shaped small pieces. Weed out any clumps of moss that appear to be growing too fast, too tall, or too thick. Save the nice compact, slow-growing clumps.

New buds that form at the apex should all be retained (**7–17**). On the top of a miniature bonsai, it's better if you don't see fresh cut marks. Keep all these buds, and trim them into a dense mass that forms the rounded shape so often seen on older rhododendrons. The future trunk is being shaped by the well-lit bottom bud closest to the cut end. The outermost top bud would produce a very boring trunk. It will shoot straight up, and, therefore, it must be kept trimmed well back.

Here's the tree two weeks later (**7–18**). Look at the tremendous new growth. It is a common misconception that you can discourage growth by pruning back a plant. All you accomplish is an increase in growth by removing terminal buds. For miniature bonsai this phenomenon is ideal. By regularly pinching back new buds, you can actually thicken growth and generate even more new buds.

Pinch out unwanted growth throughout the growing season; the sooner, the better (**7–19**). These tweezers enable the grower to select the best growth by removing the competition.

Here's the same miniature bonsai after just a few months of training (**7–20**). Notice now how the trunk appears so stout as compared to the same trunk in **7–5**. Notice also how the branches are shorter, more compact and refined, and how they contribute to the illusion of age. This miniature bonsai is now only 6 inches tall but it sports a nice 2½-inch trunk. I hope you can see how this is superior to **7–5**, where this same 2½-inch trunk was on a 16-inch bonsai. This is one of the clear advantages of miniature bonsai over their larger and taller counterparts, a greater illusion of age.

7–17

7–18

7–19

7—20

A Miniature Landscape from Cuttings

The plant we'll use is a year-old cutting of andelyensis cypress, *Chamaecyparis thyoides* 'Andelyensis Conica' (**7–21**). The growth habit of this variety assumes the shape of a miniature tree without any pruning. The plant in this photograph has never been pruned.

By trimming away some lower branches, we can age this miniature tree (**7–22**). Older specimens of most trees have lost their bottom limbs, and we can achieve this same illusion by using pruning tools.

The trimmed tree now has a more mature and refined appearance (**7–23**). A potential miniature bonsai container is shown to its right. Notice the color. The brown earth tone complements the nice green foliage associated with conifers in general.

The completed planting (**7–24**) shows the trunk of the tree just off center for an artistic display. There is not much else one can do with a small, formal upright miniature bonsai. I personally find this type of planting quite boring, however. Let's try to put some excitement into the planting by combining two more trees and a rock.

Here we have three trees instead of just one (**7–25**). We can arrange these around a red lava rock to create movement and interest. The tray is a small saikei pot of brick red *tokoname* ware from Japan.

Even though these trees are only a year old, the illusion of age is quite pronounced (**7–26**). Most viewers would guess that they were at least 10 years old in this planting. In **7–24** the single tree might have an estimated age of only 3 or 4 years.

7–21

7–22

7–23

7–24

7–25

7–26

If the combining of miniature bonsai adds to their perceived age, what happens when we carry this tendency to an extreme? Let's try planting twenty-five 1-year-old cuttings among five lava rocks (**7–27**). The pot is a homemade cedar planter box nailed together using strips of trim molding.

Place a generous amount of bonsai soil in the container (**7–28**). This will help position the rocks at the desired level. Without this soil, rocks tend to be placed with their flattest sides down because that is the only way they are stable. With plenty of soil in the pot first, you can position the rocks without regard to their most

stable flat surfaces, making it possible to assemble greater combinations and relationships.

Of course these rocks could be assembled in any number of ways. I played with them for about half an hour before this particular natural bridge formation caught my eye (**7–29**).

By adding these twenty-five cypress trees, we can form a nice landscape (**7–30**). I also added miniature ground cover and moss. There was even room for three elm trees near the cave entrance. Look how much enjoyment you can get out of cuttings that are just a year old.

7–27

7–29

7–28

7–30

CREATING MINIATURE BONSAI FROM NURSERY STOCK

In **7–31** a 2-gallon plastic nursery container holds a 16-inch *Acer ginnala*, or amur maple. It should be immediately obvious why I chose this plant for creating a miniature bonsai. Many maples continually sprout from the base or from latent buds along the trunk. Just be choosy. Select a maple that already looks mostly finished. With this candidate, only one cut will be necessary.

Four miniature bonsai pots shown in **7–32** are possible containers for the finished planting. Always have an assortment of sizes close at hand when transplanting miniatures. Sometimes a slightly larger pot is necessary. Other times, you might find that a smaller container is

7–32

7–33

7–31

not only sufficient in size, but it makes the bonsai look better as well.

A preliminary rough cut gets the tall unstable part of the tree out of the way for root-pruning purposes (**7–33**). You can always go back later and cut more precisely. For now, it is just nice to get all that foliage out of the way.

With a root hook, carefully comb the roots out away from the trunk in a radial fashion (**7–34**). Lightly tug on the handle as you work. Sharp pulls or sudden motions will damage the tiny, sensitive root hairs you're exposing.

Try to remove large roots below the soil surface while maintaining smaller productive root hairs (**7–35**). This larger root can be cut off only because of the great number of tiny roots that will remain attached closer to the root buttress.

Try the plant in the pot often (**7–36**). There should be sufficient room for fresh soil to be added to the root ball. This small black pot is going to be large enough. Looking back at **7–32**, it seems hardly possible.

Incorporate as much bonsai soil as you can into the root mass by gently pushing with a chopstick (**7–37**). Keep pushing fresh soil into the container for ten minutes to assure that there are no hidden air pockets. Wipe off the excess soil with a soft brush, then water well.

Now is a good time to carefully trim away all the excess wood that projects beyond the new apex (**7–38**). Use the spherical knob cutter to nibble away until the surface is nicely smooth and angled away from the viewer. Apply a good wound sealer to prevent damage to your new apex. A large scar like this might die back too far, and then you would have to wait for new buds to form farther down the trunk. Using a wound sealer makes it possible to safely cut very close to the new apex without damaging it.

This miniature bonsai maple (**7–39**), made only an hour ago, has great potential. Obviously the foliage is presently too large and the number of leaves is too few, but this will be corrected automatically by the plant as it starts to grow again. The trunk taper is good and the root buttress is strong-looking. These are the hardest characteristics to develop on miniature bonsai. Dwarf foliage is the easiest.

7–34

7–35

7–36

7-37

7-38

7-39

MINIATURE BONSAI FROM THE GARDEN

The mugo pine, *Pinus mugo mugo* in **7–40**, obtained from a nursery, was planted in the garden to thicken the trunk, then repotted in this black plastic container. It has been given full sun, plenty of water, and unlimited fertilizer. The only thing restricting its growth is a pruning tool and this container.

Here are possible containers (**7–41**) next to the tree in the black gallon-size container to give you an idea of sizes of pots to look for. Notice the earth colors of all the containers.

The long branch coming to the left is trimmed off (**7–42**). It is so heavy that it might be mistaken for the trunk. Then the compacted roots are pulled apart and the tree is inserted into a miniature bonsai pot.

This tree is already looking quite nice in a smaller pot (**7–43**). The small pot makes the trunk look more important. Trim the roots until the plant comfortably fits in the pot. Do not trim off too many or too few. Keep in mind that you must retain enough roots to support the foliage.

Put fresh bonsai soil over the top of the roots and push the soil particles into the root mass with chopsticks (**7–44**). Make sure that all air pockets are removed. Continue thrusting soil into the container until no more soil will fit. Then trim off small surface roots that keep popping up, brush away excess soil with a soft brush, and water well.

The *mame* bonsai in **7–45** will bud back profusely next year. The simple upright design accentuates the gentle curves of the trunk. This tree will need further root pruning next year.

7–40

7–41

7–42

7–43

7–44

7–45

Miniature Bonsai from Crab Apple Seed

The crab apple *Malus floribunda*, shown in **7–46**, was grown for three years in this container from seed collected from a bonsai crab apple. It's a healthy green and large-leaved tree in this large container, but it has superior fruit and flowers.

These four glazed vessels are possible containers (**7–47**). Notice the use of brighter pots to complement a brighter tree.

Since a good bit of the soil was quite compact, I washed most of it away with the hose (**7–48**). It is difficult to trim roots grown in sandy soil because the sand tends to ruin the sharp cutting edge of the pruning shears. A quick wash of water removes these gritty particles so that it's not only safer for tools, but it's easier to see what you're doing. This upper root should be removed to level the root buttress. A single protruding root will not contribute to the visual stability of the planting. If this root is removed now, the remaining roots will pick up the slack.

This bonsai already looks comfortable in its new container (**7–49**). The leaves are still too large and they tend to hide the beautiful apples underneath which are just now starting to turn from yellow to red. If we trim off some of the larger leaves, we can encourage new, smaller leaf buds for next year and enjoy the apples now.

Trim halfway between the leaf and the branch on the leaf stem (**7–50**). There is no need to trim closer to the branch. The remaining bit of leaf petiole will drop off in about a week as the new leaf bud under it expands. We can start to see some apples now.

This *mame* bonsai has a nice natural slant to the trunk and rootage (**7–51**). The branches are still quite short due to the recent pruning of the larger leaves, but they will come back very nicely this spring. Notice how a blue glaze complements the red crab apples.

7-46

7-47

7-48

7-49

7-50

7-51

ACCOMPANIMENT PLANTINGS

No miniature bonsai collection is complete without a few accompaniment plantings. In the traditional Japanese home the primary display shelf, the *tokonoma*, usually boasts the favorite bonsai of the host. The species of display plant sends a greeting to the guest. A pine bonsai, for instance, wishes the guest long life. In addition to this bonsai, a miniature bonsai such as grass, bulbs, lilies, tubers, and the like accompanies the display. A pine bonsai might have an accompaniment *shitakusa* planting of pine mushrooms. A third element in the display might be a watercolor scroll of the pine islands of Matsushima. The combination of these three elements increases the visual strength and meaning of the display. Where there could have been just a single bonsai on a shelf, a suggested landscape now appears with its accompanying stories and greetings for the guest. Let's make some of these plantings. They are quick and easy to grow and often capture the most smiles at a bonsai show.

This plant is unmistakably a Venus flytrap (**7–52**). As is, it's an attention-getter. In a bonsai pot next to a large swamp cypress or bog rosemary, it is quite a conversation starter. The containers in **7–53** will complement the basic green color of the plant. The smaller pots will make the "traps" seem even more significant. Trim away any unneeded, repetitive, or old areas of the plant (**7–54**). Encourage new growth by keeping the plant well watered, regularly fertilized, and temperature stable.

See how interesting this species can be (**7–55**). Notice that the number of stems has been reduced. Sometimes just a few well-placed branches makes a stronger statement than a great number of branches that seem to clutter the scene.

7–53

7–54

7–55

7–52

The popular indoor bonsai plant in **7–56** is known as Chinese snow rose, *Serissa foetida*. A plant and container this size are commonly found in most florist shops or indoor nurseries. Three possible containers are shown next to the plant (**7–57**). Serissa enjoy a very stable environment in which to grow. So for most purposes, the larger pot on the left will make this planting easy to care for. The smaller pots will make the miniature bonsai tree look older. In transplanting this bonsai (**7–58**), I discovered many more roots that could be exposed, making it necessary to tilt the plant a bit and turn it around to the other side. The completed planting is quite old-looking (**7–59**), compared with the plant started with in **7–56**. This miniature bonsai will bloom for ten months of the year with the cutest little white flowers that look like miniature roses.

7–58

7–56

7–57

7–59

The *Dionaea muscipula* 'Sandersonii' (**7–60**), like the Venus flytrap above, is also a carnivorous plant. The sticky sweet residues on the obscure foliage attract small gnats which then get stuck on the leaves. Eventually, the insect body decomposes and is absorbed by the plant, much like what happens inside the jaws of the flytrap above. Potential containers (**7–61**) for these marvelous tiny white flowers include a porcelain and cloisonné brass container. A brightly colored pot such as this would have to have a drain hole drilled in the bottom. For now, I'll select the small black pot.

The sharp contrast of black and white make this a striking accompaniment planting (**7–62**). Try an arrangement with a banyan or tropical fig. This planting would look great with a scroll of poetry in *sumi* ink on rice paper.

7–60

7–61

7–62

The succulent in **7–63** is *Euphorbia decaryl*, a plant which resembles a palm tree in miniature; so, I thought it might make an interesting miniature bonsai. Three possible pots are shown in photo **7–64**. An earth brown color would be better than a bright glaze, considering the color of the succulent. Photo **7–65** shows the completed planting. The lower side shoots were retained to form a cluster of tree-like shapes. Observe how the bonsai pot complements the gentle curves of the plants. Use this miniature as an accompaniment planting to go with high-desert juniper bonsai.

7–63

7–64

7–65

The interesting plant in **7–66** is *Trichodiadema bulbosum*, another dry-climate form. The bulb at the base gives one the impression of an expanded root buttress. An assortment of appropriate pots is shown in **7–67** next to the plant for comparative purposes.

Notice how the branches can look quite dramatic when they all lean to one side (**7–68**). I realize that this is not windswept material, but I think the design is more interesting this way than straight up.

7–66

7–67

7–68

The plant in **7–69** is a common find in most florist shops, Ming aralia, or *Polyscias fruticosa*. There is nothing spectacular about this specimen. I just wanted to illustrate an earlier point that a few well placed branches look better than a crowded, full-foliage tree. First, let's transfer this mediocre bonsai (**7–70**) from its plastic pot and get it into a nice ceramic pot. The rounded corners of this bonsai container will complement the rounded curves of the plant. Once you transplant, move the rock over to the new pot as well (**7–71**). We will dispense with the bright gravel, however. Next, let's concentrate on pruning the top to accentuate the nice natural curves in the trunk and foliage.

I hope you can see that the few remaining branches are well placed and distinct (**7–72**). The tree appears more to be like a miniature version of an older specimen. Its crown is distinct and there is visible trunk movement. Compare this photograph to **7–69**. Isn't this better?

7–70

7–69

7–71

CREATING MINIATURE BONSAI
117

Here in **7-73** is another example of an extremely common plant in an uncommon use as a miniature bonsai. It is an asparagus fern, *Asparagus plumosa*. Here in **7-74** are a variety of containers that would work well with this fern. Let's transplant it and try to arrange a nice lacy visual effect by pruning out the congested growth. Notice in **7-75** how the light picks up the individual fronds now that the design is simplified. This miniature bonsai would look well with any wet-weather or tropical bonsai.

7-73

7-74

7-75

Since one does not normally think of bonsai ferns, I'd like to do one more for you to try to convince you how versatile and beautiful they can be. This plant is a common rabbit's-foot fern, *Davallia fejeenis* (**7–76**). Three suggested containers are shown next to the nursery plant (**7–77**). I hope that by showing you these pots with all these plants, you can start to see how easy their selection can be. Again, as with the previous fern, see how a few well-placed fronds make the miniature planting more striking (**7–78**). The aerial roots on this plant resemble rabbits' feet both visually and tactilely, hence the common name.

7–76

7–77

7–78

7–79

7–80

Here (see **7–79**) is a fairly common plant in a very uncommon use. It is redwood sorrel, *Oxalis oregana*, a shade plant for the garden. These pots (**7–80**) seem to go well with this clover-like plant. Oxalis has a nice small white flower in spring. Here is another good example of a dramatic pruning job (**7–81**). I realize that oxalis is not a windswept plant. I am just trying to achieve some visual interest in an otherwise symmetrical plant.

7–81

Let's try an herb, 'Bressingham', a thyme hybrid (**7–82**). This nice, tight creeping plant naturally cascades over this nursery pot; so, let's make a miniature cascading bonsai out of it. Nice pink flowers will appear. The three pots in **7–83** are all cascading pots, obviously. The bright blue pot will look best when the thyme is in bloom; otherwise it will be a bit harsh in color. So, let's try the plain reddish brown pot instead.

As it turns out, the best way to direct the growth was to the right (**7–84**). This required turning the plant's back toward the front and realigning the small leaves with a few days of sunlight from the right side.

7–82

7–83

7–84

No book on miniature bonsai would be complete without mention of mondo grass, *Ophiopogon japonicus* (**7–85**). This is perhaps the most widely used plant for accompanying larger bonsai. Perhaps that's because it is so easy to plant, or because it looks so well with most species of larger bonsai. The shallow containers shown in **7–86** will complement the narrow blades of grass. Thicker, taller, or heavier pots would overwhelm the lacy nature of the blades of grass.

Most grasses, when allowed to grow untrimmed from year to year, will peak up on their root structure (**7–87**). This is what makes old fescue fields so bumpy. A good bonsai design mimics nature; so, when you plant your grasses, including bamboo, mound them up, to add age to their appearance.

7–85

7–86

7–87

Here's one last project. I would like to show you the development of a miniature pink rhododendron, *Rhododendron kiusianum* (**7–88**). This old plant was dug from a yard where it was no longer wanted. It is approximately twenty-five years old, with a 4½-inch trunk that barely fits into this 5-inch pot. The next photo (**7–89**) shows how this plant looked just the following spring after a severe pruning. It is going to be one of my favorite miniature bonsai.

I hope that this chapter inspires you to create your own miniature bonsai. They are so much fun and so easy! I enjoyed the excuse of shopping for plants and pots so that I could make them for this book. Visitors admire these simple creations almost as much as the larger, older bonsai I have. I urge you to try them. The plantings are so quick that you have more time to spend on design, and a wider range of species is available and appropriate than for larger bonsai.

7–88

7–89

CREATING MINIATURE BONSAI

8

CARE &
MAINTENANCE

INDOORS OR OUTDOORS?

The biggest problem in basic bonsai care may be whether to grow bonsai indoors or outdoors. Well-meaning individuals may try to grow a juniper bonsai on their coffee table. A pine tree slowly withers on top of the television set. A florist azalea turns black on the picnic table outside. If you buy a bonsai, pay careful attention to the location in which it was growing. If you have any questions, ask the shopkeeper. Additional growing information is usually provided with the plant as a handout, brochure, or instruction label. Read these materials carefully. If questions remain in your mind, contact a member of a local bonsai society or garden club.

With the burgeoning interest in bonsai comes a variety of available bonsai. "Bonsai" are now made of silk, paper, silver wire, plastic, and other sturdy materials. This new product, quite convincing in appearance, is a preserved plant. Typically a juniper, this bonsai appears quite green and flexible and is usually planted in a plastic bonsai container. A naïve customer or gift recipient might actually believe that this plant will thrive and grow. These bonsai are quite dead already and should not be confused with living models. Again, if you question the plant's authenticity, ask the establishment where you bought it. If you received it as a gift, surreptitiously ask a knowledgeable gardener friend.

With a variety of stores supplying bonsai and bonsai material, it becomes imperative to be able to positively identify the plant. If you don't know the plant species, you won't know how to care for the plant. I have seen bonsai sold at outdoor markets, grocery stores, department stores, and variety shops. So, bonsai is placed on a shelf temporarily while for sale. But such a spot is probably not the best environment for its successful growth.

Common names should be avoided if at all possible. A Norfolk Island pine is not a pine. A *hinoki* cypress is not a cypress. A Chinese snow rose is not a rose. There are countless more examples where the common name for a plant is misleading. For this reason, most serious gardeners use the Latin name. Also, to ensure accurate information for the reader, most books refer to the Latin designation wherever practical.

The plant lists for outdoor bonsai, partially outdoor bonsai, and indoor bonsai include common names of most of the larger groups of plants suitable for bonsai. These lists are by no means complete.

Outdoor Bonsai

Outdoor bonsai are typically conifers, broadleaf evergreens, and deciduous trees, found native to the colder parts of our planet. These hardy trees and shrubs are subject to freezing temperatures every winter in their natural habitats. As bonsai, they tolerate some freezing temperatures overnight. The variety of plants in this classification is large, accounting for most bonsai species. Included in this group are pine, juniper, hemlock, spruce, fir, cedar, rhododendron, azalea, alder, hornbeam, birch, beech, camellia, quince, dogwood, redbud, cypress, hawthorn, larch, filbert, cherry, pear, oak, willow, and arborvitae.

Partially Outdoor Bonsai

Partially outdoor bonsai are native to temperate climates of the globe. While it may sometimes freeze in their local environment, it is not necessary that the potted tree be subject to these cold temperatures. Bonsai growers typically move the plant about as climatic changes dictate. The bonsai is placed outdoors in April in the shade. It spends the summer cooling in the breezes under the canopy of a large tree. When the first frosts of fall arrive, the tree becomes an indoor bonsai, in a sunny location in the home. In the spring, the cycle continues. Some good examples of these plants are evergreen oaks, evergreen maples, Chinese elm, Japanese green mound juniper, Kingsbury boxwood, Chinese tea, pomegranate, bamboo, Montezuma cypress, bald cypress, buttonwood, peach, citrus, jade, succulent pine, fuchsia, magnolia, olive, palm, *seiju* elm, *hokkaido* elm, Chinese snow rose, and Chinese date tree.

Indoor Bonsai

Indoor bonsai are made from tropical plants. Typical florist shops handle these indoor plants native to the equatorial regions of Africa, Asia, and South America. Small-leaved varieties are most often used rather than those with enormous leaves found in lush rain forests. The bonsai is usually placed in a well-lit location with adequate ventilation. In warmer climates, these bonsai can be brought outside for limited duration in full shade. Some plants often utilized are figs, shefflera, aralia, cycas, kalanchoe, pelargonium, succulents, cacti, portulacaria, hibiscus, fatshedera, crassula, hedera, nerium, pilea, poinsettia and bougainvillea.

Although most bonsai exhibitions are found indoors, most bonsai are outdoor or partially outdoor plants. If

the lives of his masterpieces, the bonsai of his grandfather and the bonsai of his future grandchildren. Watering is by no means a small task to be taken lightly. With a careful eye to the moisture content in the container, you can control growth, inhibit insects, prevent disease, and monitor the general development of your tree. Water is not simply wetness in the pot; it's indeed the lifeblood of the plant. Water carries nutrients, helps the plant breathe in summer, and transports growth hormones. It provides the turgor pressure necessary to keep new growth upright. Water keeps the plant flexible so that it can turn toward the sun and align itself with the seasons. Water provides the transportation for a universe of biochemical processes without which all systems fail. Osmosis between living cells ceases without water.

Plants growing in the ground have a large volume from which to draw their necessary moisture. The containerized plant has no such reserve to draw upon. Once the bonsai is dry, it is desperately dry. The plant in the ground can rely on deeper roots for sustenance in warmer weather. The volume of a bonsai pot simply does not allow for a so-called taproot. This is why careful attention to watering bonsai is so critical. By confining the roots in an enclosed container, you commit yourself to providing the plant with all its needs. If that obligation is too demanding on your time and attention, simply plant the bonsai in the ground for a few days or a few years as your personal needs dictate. The bonsai can always be repotted later. Better a live potential bonsai growing in the ground than a dead bonsai in a beautiful pot.

Three-Step Watering

First, water your bonsai lightly, then leave the bonsai alone for ten or fifteen minutes. Continuous watering at this point is futile and wasted. The dryness of the soil particles creates a repulsion to water due to the surface tension of the water itself. The soil particles as well as the container are able to make the water microscopically bead up and be temporarily rejected. After a few minutes this surface tension relaxes as the soil particles become wetted. Later, the soil is ready to receive additional moisture. A good, thorough sprinkling or soaking at this time drenches the soil particles, and the moisture content in the soil reaches almost 100 percent. All soil particles are wetted. The inside as well as the outside of the container is wet. The excess water flows freely through the drain holes and air is sucked

you want an indoor bonsai, simply pot and train an indoor plant. If you purchase a finished bonsai, make sure you're aware of its needs. A tropical plant from the equator does not have to feel the seasons since there are none in its native habitat. If only needs lots of indirect light, consistent moisture, and moderate heat. Outdoor plants, by contrast, need to feel the passage of the seasons to set their internal biological clocks. They depend heavily on the height, location, and duration of the sun to create winter, spring, summer, and fall, just as all plants do that are native to colder parts of the globe.

WATERING

When my bonsai teacher finally handed me his watering can after months of training, I knew I had graduated. With that simple gesture, he was trusting me with

down from above by the action of the retreating water as it channels through the soil.

After this **second watering**, an important process occurs that takes about ten minutes. The flood of water in the soil dislodges dust, fills minor crevices, and dissolves minerals and salts in the soil. During this period of time, an equilibrium is reached. The osmotic pressure around the soil particles begins to equal the osmotic pressure inside the root hairs of the plant. Ion exchange begins and the botanical machinery starts to function. Waste products are disposed of and nutrient stores are inventoried and adjusted. Storage organs are cleaned and purged of unnecessary or redundant supplies.

A **third watering** is a bonus to the plant. Excess mineral byproducts and harmful salts are disposed of rapidly in the presence of water-saturated soil. A dry soil will force the plant to retain these harmful wastes. By watering a third time you do not increase the moisture content in the soil significantly. You accomplish something more important: you take out the garbage. Miss this third watering, and your plant will not perform well. Make a point of watering this critical third time.

Water content of the soil gradually decreases toward zero. This is due to evaporation, transpiration within the plant itself, and, of course, the growth of the root tips. In any case, there comes to be insufficient water in the pot available to the plant. Although some residual moisture is still left in the pot, it is of no use to the plant.

Water Quality and Watering Cans

One aspect of watering often ignored is attention to the quality of water. If after several months of careful watering you still see white mineral deposits accumulated on the inside rim of the pot, you may have a highly mineral water supply. You'll have to store your water before utilizing it. A large water vessel of some kind can be used to settle out minerals and evaporate high amounts of chlorine and related elements. Standing water is always safer for bonsai than water directly from the tap or well. In Japanese nurseries they dip a traditional copper watering can into a large ceramic or oak vessel, and carry the water to each individual plant. For convenience and comfort, we often use other sources. However, if your water seems to be having an adverse effect on your trees, governmental agencies can test it, usually for a modest fee. Sometimes prior storage is the simplest solution.

Hoses, Nozzles, and Systems

For most purposes, however, tap water from a hose seems to be the watering method of choice. There are watering nozzles available from nurseries that spread the water out into fine droplets that do not harm the plant or wash away the soil. The rose at the end of the Japanese bonsai watering can has been modified for hose-end use. This is what I prefer. There are also countless watering devices with built-in shutoff valves and pressure regulators on the market. Try to select one that best suits your individual needs and applications. For the smallest of miniature bonsai, you may find it useful to use a syringe (**8–1**).

Numerous automated systems are available to make your bonsai watering schedule interfere less with your social schedule. These systems have several things in common. They are more expensive than simple nozzles, watering cans, or sprinklers. They require planning and installation, and they all fail at some time or another. Nurseries with elaborate watering systems costing tens of thousands of dollars still have to call the plumber once in a while. An automatic watering system can be a useful tool if approached with mechanical knowledge, constant observation, and humor. If a squirrel decides that your miniature water emitter is in its way, it will simply move it out of the way. If your bonsai dies subsequently, it was not the squirrel's fault, it was because you did not get out and observe your system closely enough. You trusted it to do your work for you.

Pipes freeze, water lines burst, fittings leak, solenoids fail, and electricity may be interrupted. Ultimately, the responsibility and success of your watering schedule

8–1

still depends upon you. Quiet time with my trees is something I look forward to. For some, I suppose bonsai is an inconvenience. But then there are others like me.

WEEDING

Normally one would not think that weeding, or more specifically, lack of weeding, could seriously affect the life of a bonsai. Weeds are just plants that we wish would grow somewhere else. Unfortunately, the most prolific and well-known weeds are those plants that can compete successfully with what we try to grow. If we nurture our bonsai properly, we will eventually find a weed in the pot that grows just fine under those conditions. It is important to remove these pests as soon as possible while their root systems are still small. Once a major weed, such as a thistle, gets its roots tangled up with your favorite pine bonsai roots, it will be necessary to repot the whole tree. Otherwise the thistle will regrow in just a few days.

Weeds compete favorably with bonsai. They rob nutrition from the soil that's intended for the tree. They shade the roots of the bonsai, which causes the bonsai to sulk. They detract from the appearance of the planting. They harbor insects and disease, even attracting them to the site. They throw off your watering schedule by growing quickly.

Some weeds indicate poor soil conditions. The common liverwort appears only when certain environmental circumstances are present. When you see this weed, look for poor-draining soil. Check to see that there is no rotting humus in your soil, clogging its breathing pores. This weed is often seen when high nitrogen fertilizers or time-release capsules have been applied to the soil surface. A word of caution: time-release fertilizers are dependent on higher temperatures as well as time. Heavy application of these fertilizers to the soil surface without adequate water flushing will encourage formation of green slime. Liverwort thrives in such an environment.

Irish moss and its close companion, Scotch moss, make nice ground covers in the garden. Their colors range from a bright chartreuse to a deep, grassy green. Their petite white flowers make them irresistible to bonsai fanciers. But do not be tempted. The roots of both types of mosses will go to the bottom of a 5-inch-deep bonsai pot. Once established, they become the weeds that will test your persistence. Sometimes the

only way to get rid of them is to totally bare-root your bonsai. At first sign of these pesky weeds, get your tweezers out and remove them immediately, being sure to dig deep.

Most weeds, fortunately, are the kind that you might have in your lawn or vegetable garden. These are easily plucked out with the tweezers when they are young. Larger specimens can still be teased out gently with the hands.

Bonsai plants that require frequent watering have frequent weeds. A recently deposited weed seed has a greater chance of getting a nice timely shower after landing on a bonsai that's watered frequently. If you have trouble with common weeds on the soil surface of your juniper or alpine fir, I suspect that you're simply watering your bonsai whether it needs it or not. When I water with a watering can, I water only those plants that need it. When I water with a hose, I tend to water

everything just because it's so easy. This bad habit tends to promote weeds.

A popular ground cover known as baby's tears seems to make its way into bonsai pots. This invasive plant will take over a bonsai planting in just a few months. Getting rid of it takes just as long. Beware of this innocuous-looking plant with the cherubic name.

Just as a good, healthy, and compact lawn will resist weeds, a compact moss under your bonsai will help cut down on vegetative pests. I prefer the low type of silvery gray green moss that grows on stones and concrete. I grind up a bit of the moss between my fingers and sprinkle it on the soil surface. Most of the spores do not survive, but it only takes a few starts to achieve the effect you want. Do not allow moss to cover your whole pot. Too much moss becomes a weed in itself.

SUMMER CARE

Chapter 2 covered many of the aspects of watering; however, summer presents unique problems. Regulating water in a container requires coordinating three main factors.

First, the size of the container. As the width and depth of the container doubles, the volume contained increases geometrically. For example, a square pot 1 inch on a side contains only 1 cubic inch of soil. By contrast, a square pot that's 2 inches on each side contains 8 cubic inches of soil. Presuming the first container will dry out in an hour, it's possible that the second larger container will dry out after only eight hours. That makes the large pot the better choice for a working person. Do not be afraid to pot your bonsai a little bigger if you have difficulty keeping them moist.

Second, shade probably affects a plant's moisture content more than any other factor. If your bonsai container is drying out in four hours, move it to a shadier location. By observing the sun's path across the growing area, you can learn where the hot spots are and where the temperature naturally remains cooler.

Third, you can regulate your watering frequency. It may be necessary for you to water both morning and evening rather than to water only in the morning and have some trees suffer all night long. In summer, lack of water is the most serious mistake one can make.

You'll have to make constant adjustments to your watering schedule, depending on the temperature, humidity, season, location, health of plant, age of tree, degree it's pot-bound, vigor of species, prevailing wind, length of day, altitude, type of planting, and styling considerations. Let's consider how each of these factors affects your summer care schedule.

Temperature

If you want to know when to repot your pine, just schedule repotting around the time of your local summer fair, when it's sure to rain. A few nice, cool days precede the downpour, so that makes it perfect summer weather to transplant, repot, or defoliate your maples. Always use plenty of water when transplanting during the summer. Not all summers are created equal. A few years back, my water bill actually exceeded my electric bill due to the unusual demand. Make adjustments as necessary.

Humidity

Plants feel humidity as well as humans. High humidity means that it's difficult to shed excess moisture. For plants, that means mildew and fungus. When the weather is overcast, warm, and muggy, I advise mildew protection for some sensitive species—crab apple, cotoneaster, pyracantha, rose, plum, prune, peach, almond, and pear. A light application of fungicide will protect them from leaf curl, blight, black spot, rust, and powdery mildew. It is far easier to target susceptible trees and treat them while healthy than to wait for them to be infected and try to cure them in that weakened condition.

The Season

I am very much aware of different seasons around the world. My early training in bonsai was from a Japanese book while in Japan. I soon discovered that Japanese seasonal tasks took into account that it was dry in the winter and wet in the summer. Where I now live, in the northwestern United States, it is wet in the winter and dry in the summer. Seasonal adjustments had to be made.

Location

By *location* I mean specific location in your growing area, not the geographical sense. If you have a nice, cool area in your backyard where you like to sit, you might consider this an excellent place for your Japanese maples. They enjoy morning sun, but when the temperature starts to rise in the afternoon, they like to relax under the canopy of a large shade tree with their favorite beverage, water. If on the other hand, your patio faces south and basks in the warm sun every afternoon, you should be able to grow the finest pine and juniper bonsai possible. People whose yards are completely shaded with mature trees would envy this opportunity. Take advantage of location attributes. Grow what's easiest for you. Remember, what's easy for you might be very difficult for another.

Health of Plant

A tree that has a problem will appear different from its neighbors. This difference is actually easier to see from a distance. Close up, one cannot accurately compare color to healthy adjacent plants. The first sign of difficulty is that the stressed tree lacks clarity in color. It is almost as if you are looking through a semitransparent screen surrounding the tree. The green colors fade slightly to gray. The clarity of foliage detail appears out of focus. More obvious, the plant starts using water at a *decreased* rate as compared to its close neighbors. When this happens time is of the essence. A quick shower of systemic fungicide, moving the tree away from the shade and shelter of other plants, and restricting water will usually save the plant. By the time the foliage starts to fall off, it is too late. Be aware of your plant's normal activity. A sudden change in color or a sudden change in water uptake could indicate a serious problem. If you water everything with a sprinkler whether it needs it or not, you miss an early warning.

Age of Tree

A recently transplanted tree should have the protection of full shade for at least ten days. Water these plants every day, even though they're not drying out. In two weeks the transplant will start growing vigorously. After this time, apply a low-nitrogen fertilizer to stimulate it further. An actively growing plant should use a tremendous amount of water as it grows. As a bonsai ages, it requires a bit less water and a bit more shade. Let's compare two plants, a 5-year-old trident maple bonsai and a 50-year-old trident maple bonsai. The younger plant can use more fertilizer as it grows to maturity. It will use moisture rapidly as it develops. Moisture consumption will be great if its proportional size is taken into consideration. Its leaves will be large, and it will tolerate full sun most of the day. The older maple of the same variety will have smaller leaves and

appreciate full shade around two o'clock in the afternoon. Its growth will be slower than the younger's. It will require less fertilizer, and in spite of it being a grand old tree, its water uptake will be proportionately reduced. Take these factors into consideration when taking care of older specimens. They will appreciate it.

Degree of Being Pot-Bound

Just what does *pot-bound* mean? I like to think in terms of percentages. If a bonsai container contains half roots and half soil, I call this 50 percent pot-bound. Good bonsai practice allows the percentage of roots to go as high as 90 percent without sustaining permanent damage to the bonsai. To be sure, such a plant requires repotting immediately. (See chapter 7.) A bonsai that's 50 percent pot-bound is going to stay wet longer than a bonsai that's 90 percent pot-bound, even though both

plants are the same size. By watching a plant's sun and shade tolerance and observing water uptake, you can predict the pot-bound percentage. If a pine tree uses up moisture quickly in spite of being placed in the shade, check its roots. It is probably badly pot-bound and could use repotting into a larger container. All summer long, make mental notes of these schedules. Irregularities in these schedules could mean that further investigation is necessary.

Vigor of Species

Obviously, a willow is going to require more water than a pine. Species like birch, beech, hornbeam, elm, and alder are also thirsty plants. Because the elm is a thirsty plant, water its foliage as well as the pot. This will help clean off the leaves as well as provide additional moisture. Mountain and desert conifers use water sparingly; so, give them a sunny location and water only when necessary. Avoid watering their foliage. They are not used to it in nature; so, try to duplicate that in your backyard.

Prevailing Wind

Wind velocity decreases as you approach ground level. The same principle applies as you approach trees, fences, or houses. If you bonsai dry out too fast, you may have too much wind. Try moving the bonsai closer to the ground or tuck it in under the canopy of tree or the eaves of a house. If a tree has trouble drying out, move it out a little more into the open, or elevate it on a high shelf. Excessively windy areas may require construction of a shelter or windbreak. Usually it's best to protect bonsai on at least two sides in a windy area.

Length of Day

As spring progresses toward summer, the sun rises earlier, gains a steep angle toward noon, and finally sets. The length of the day, temperature, and steep angle of the sun make a stressful day for unprotected bonsai. As the days get even longer, you'll find sun on the north side of your home, both morning and evening. Shade plants left there unprotected can burn easily. The steep angle of the sun severely reduces the area of shade cast by a tree. So watch to make sure your bonsai benches are protected during hot afternoons.

Altitude

Skiers and mountain climbers know that extra protection from the sun is necessary at higher elevations. Plants feel the force of high ultraviolet radiation as well. If you live above 3,000 feet in altitude, appropriate adjustments should be made. Above 4,000 feet even greater caution should be taken with low-altitude native plant material. For example, if a Japanese maple tolerates summer sun from dawn until 2 P.M. at sea level, at 4,000 feet the same maple must be in full shade by noon to prevent damage.

Type of Planting

Perhaps the easiest style of bonsai to take care of is the semicascade style. It is always planted in a big square pot that's not too tall, so that it doesn't tip over in a wind gust. The lower branch does not scrape on the bench or hang over the edge of the bench as in the cascade style. The pot is easy to water, drains well for its size, and yet retains moisture well during hot days. Cascade pots tend to tip over, whether from cats, birds, wind, or squirrels. Their small openings require an extra effort to ensure that adequate moisture reaches the roots. These pots drain exceptionally well.

The formal upright style has a tendency to stay wet too long because wide lower branches shade the surface of the roots. Also, shallow containers do not drain as well as deep containers. Turn a wet sponge on its end and it will dry out rapidly. Leave it flat and it takes a long time to dry out. The same principle holds true for the shapes of bonsai pots. The most troublesome style to take care of in summer is the rock planting. The small volume of soil, plus the increased wind exposure, create a constant watering problem. Run a large piece of cord or lantern wick up the back side of your rock planting and fasten it in several places securely to your soil mass with pins or staples. Place the lower end of the wick in a glass of water. The wick will carry water from the glass to the planting by capillary action. This is, of course, not suitable for show, but it works for dry summers. Small bonsai need water several times a day due to their small containers.

Styling Considerations

All designs are based on strengthening the tree's attributes and weakening the tree's deficiencies. If your tree is weak, underdeveloped, spindly, or has a small trunk, the best favor you can do to promote its style is to pull it from the pot and plant it in the ground for the summer. Practice your potting skills on a bonsai that's more highly developed. It makes little sense to stress a tree, reduce its leaf size, gray its trunk, defoliate it, restrict water, adjust its fertilizer, or wire it if its trunk is only as big as a pencil. Why not plant it in the ground, put a sprinkler on it, and enjoy your summer. When summer is over, the trunk will be significantly larger in size. Your tree will be green, healthy, and happy. You can then put it back in the bonsai pot and enjoy it three other seasons of the year.

Summer is an ideal time to maintain the dead wood on your bonsai. Intentional dead tops, branches, and strips of gray on the trunk add to the illusion of age. These areas are call *jin*, *shari*, and *saba-miki*. In the summer, when it's warm and dry, a light coating of lime sulfur will help keep these areas a nice driftwood gray and combat insects and disease. Simply dip a small brush into the bottom of liquid lime sulfur and paint it on the dead areas. The initial yellow color will gray out overnight in warm weather.

WINTER CARE

Winter care deals primarily with the problems of cold. Ways to cope with this problem are as varied as your individual circumstances, local environment, and garden facilities. Some possible ways bonsai owners can protect their trees from excess cold include positioning in the yard, burying, mulching, and sheltering or heating.

Position in the Yard

Wind decreases under trees, next to a fence, or near a house foundation. We are all aware of the factor known as wind chill. Plants feel this effect as well as animals. On a freezing day, plants exposed to wind suffer. Plants protected from wind will not. Take your bonsai off their high display shelves in winter, and put them on the ground. The added protection provided is considerable. When temperatures drop below freezing, cluster your bonsai together near the foundation of your home. Not only will the wind chill be reduced, a certain amount of heat leakage from your house, no matter how slight, will also assist your trees. A simple cardboard box will help keep the bonsai out of the wind. Additional protection may be required from strong directional prevailing winds.

Burying

Just like protection from summer heat, burying or planting your bonsai in the garden protects it from moderate cold. If the outside temperature drops to 28° F for several hours, the soil surface will be frozen, but just 2 inches down, the soil remains above freezing. Remove it carefully from the pot. If you soil does not drain well, just place the bonsai on the soil surface and drag adjacent soil toward the bonsai root ball. If it snows, just push some extra snow toward your tree. It's a great insulator. This is just enough protection for most outdoor bonsai. Persistent lower temperatures require additional protection for your bonsai collection.

Mulching

First plant your bonsai (without its pot) in a convenient area of your garden out of the wind. Then push a bunch of freshly fallen leaves up against the tree trunk. Cover the whole tree if it is deciduous. Then sprinkle a bit of granular fertilizer, like 16–16–16, over the fallen leaves. An amazing thing will happen. The leaves will start to decompose in the presence of the fertilizer and then heat up. This is winter protection at its easiest and purest since this is what happens in nature, only it's more localized and rapid.

Sheltering

My local climate will freeze hard for a week every winter. The only problem is figuring out which week it's going to happen. By paying close attention to the evening news and my outside thermometer, I can anticipate an unusually severe winter storm. When this happens, I simply bring the most sensitive bonsai into my garage. Technically, it is unheated, but it is always much warmer than outside, possibly due to heat leakage from the house, the greenhouse effect from the windows, or simply because it is completely out of the wind. In any case, when the storm is over, these sensitive bonsai can go back outside and seem to suffer no ill effects from their week in partial darkness.

Serious bonsai growers usually construct a cold frame for winter protection. This consists of a below-ground pit with a wooden framework over it. Cover the gaps in the wood with glass or clear plastic sheeting. The principle is that the ground 2 feet below the surface will not freeze solid. The transparent cover captures the sun's heat and holds it inside the pit. The easiest cold frame to construct is against the foundation of your home. Incorporate a ventilating hole in the side of the foundation into the pit so that excess heat and or cold can be disbursed through that vent opening. In the event of bright winter sun, the top is cracked open slightly to avoid overheating inside. Construct the cold frame large enough to hold your entire outdoor bonsai collection.

For serious bonsai collectors or bonsai enthusiasts in very harsh winter climates, the best option is a heated greenhouse. With the use of automatic thermally controlled shutters, your bonsai area can be kept at a modest 34° F at night and allowed to heat up to 48° F during the day, a perfect winter for outdoor bonsai. This equipment is more expensive than the other methods, but if it's necessary, it's well worth it.

8–2

INSECTS

The number and variety of insects on our planet is incomprehensible. Fortunately for bonsai growers, relatively few of this vast array pose a threat. Even among those insects found on our trees, some are quite beneficial.

Soft-Bodied, Sucking Insects

This huge insect classification includes the ever-present aphid (8–2), white fly, thrip, mite, and mealybug. These insects are mobile only when they have to be. They prefer staying in one general area sucking the sap of the tree and depositing their waste, known as honeydew. They all proliferate at an astounding rate; their generation is measured in hours, not days. One aphid today means twenty aphids tomorrow; so, careful observation of your plants is most important. Fortunately, their eradication is the easiest. Slowly mix ½ teaspoon of liquid dish detergent into one quart of water in a hand spray bottle. An empty window-cleaner bottle is ideal. There's no need to use a compressed-air type of applicator. Do not shake the solution or excess foam will interfere with the siphoning action of the inner tube.

Apply this spray at dusk when the wind and temperature are down. Wet the upper and lower surfaces of the foliage until runoff begins. Especially spray onto cracks, knotholes, and surface irregularities in the bark where insects can hide at night. Reapply this solution every three days for two weeks at a minimum. Do not depend on a single application to remove all pests. Future generations of insects are already in egg form and waiting to hatch. Under the stress of insecticides, an aphid can actually give birth to hundreds of live youngsters after being sprayed the first time. The reason most so-called organic sprays don't work is usually due to the lack of the applicator's persistence. You have to be willing to exceed the insects' tenacity with careful observation and repeated applications. Do not be tempted to increase the soap concentration or overwet the plant. This only endangers the plant, not the insect.

Caterpillars

Signs of damage from caterpillars are unmistakable. Large crescent-shaped areas are missing from the edges of leaves. The caterpillar usually avoids the midrib and major veins of leaves because they are too tough to eat. Encasing itself in a rolled-up leaf with its web around it, this voracious eater may rest for the hottest part of the day and munch away again at night.

I have found that the best solution is to go out after sundown, armed with a flashlight and a pair of tweezers. Even large amounts of damage can be due to only one caterpillar. There is no need to mix toxic sprays and treat your whole bonsai collection. Just go out to find it and squash it! For the squeamish, sometimes it helps to look at your damaged leaves to get up your nerve to do this nasty deed. If your surrounding trees are loaded with caterpillars, you might have to seek professional eradication because of the danger to your bonsai of reinfestation.

Spiders

This common garden inhabitant is only trying to catch other flying insects. Don't worry. It is not eating your bonsai. The webs are unsightly and certainly should be removed from a bonsai before a show. Also, there is nothing quite like the exhilarating experience of running face first into an invisible web early in the morning in your garden. This will wake you up quicker than a cup of coffee. Excess webbing can be torn down, although most webs will be rebuilt in just a few hours. I try to keep the general level of flying insects down in my garden by clearing up wet debris, not watering in the evening, and draining off any standing water. Do not leave empty buckets or containers outside that can accumulate even minute amounts of water. These can become insect watering holes and hatcheries for mosquito larvae. Spiders build webs where food is plentiful. Take care of problem flying insects, and spiders will prefer to dine elsewhere. If you happen across a spider's nest where thousands of tiny spiders are hatching, just physically remove the nest.

Protected Pests

Good examples of this category include the spittlebug, scale insects, and woolly aphid. These insects surround themselves with a protective coating or growth. The spittlebug's bubbly film is easily washed away with a forceful stream of soapy water. The scale insect protects itself with a hard crust. The soft-bodied insect inside this crust is highly vulnerable to any insecticide. Cover the outside coating with a heavy layer of mineral oil delivered on the tip of a cotton swab (**8–3**). The oily layer suffocates the scale inhabitant. The woolly aphid

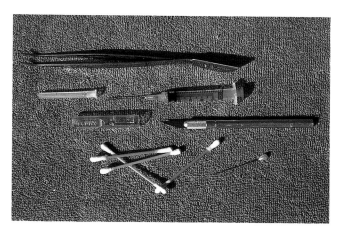

8–3

protects itself with a cotton-like substance it secretes. The minute fibers repel water and, therefore, insecticides as well. A product known to orchard farmers as spreader-sticker is the solution to this problem barrier. This product is a wetting agent and oil-based sticky substance combined. Simple detergent plus this spreader-sticker will penetrate the previously unwettable surface of the "wool," thereby eliminating the now susceptible pest. Other insect-eliminating tools in **8–3** are tweezers; a sharp, pointed knife; and a hat pin. These methods are not for the squeamish, but they avoid pesticides, a definite plus.

Boring Insects

If you see a hole in your tree about the size of a nail shank, you probably have a boring insect inside. Even antique furniture, hundreds of years old, sometimes has this problem. The insect drills a small access hole into the wood. Then it spends the rest of its life safely tucked away inside the heartwood of your valued bonsai. On dead wood, the borer is seen as a small hole. Underneath live bark, it is seen as a constantly festering ooze of sap as the tree tries to protect itself from this rude invasion. Where the entrance hole is visible, inject insecticide directly into the opening from a syringe shown in **8–3**. When the hole is obscured by the constant flow of sap, systemic treatment of the whole plant is necessary with a systemic insecticide. Follow the directions on the label, but apply only half the recommended dose to your bonsai. Better to be forced to apply a second time than have the first application damage your tree.

Slugs and Snails

These common garden pests are universal. Prized by some as escargots, they are quite repulsive to others. The damage they do occurs mainly at night when their sticky, slimy bodies move across surfaces with ease. Signs to look for in the morning include the whitish trails they leave behind. Damage to foliage is random, sometimes at the edge of a leaf like a caterpillar, but their powerful mouths can create great holes in the center of a leaf as well. They are slow-moving and can usually be found nearby lurking in the shade or moist bottom surface of the plant's container.

Both snails (**8–4**) and slugs are fond of beer, which is their downfall. Buy the least expensive brew you can find; they do not exhibit good taste in beer. Pour about

8-4

an inch into an empty tuna can and place it near the problem area. In the morning, the party will be over, and you'll have nothing but a mess to clean up.

Weevils

Just when you thought it was easy to eradicate garden pests, along comes the weevil and closely related insects. This group of insects are never seen. Even at night they're hard to see or catch, but their damage patterns are quite noticeable and characteristic. Small notches taken from the outer borders of leaves are well rounded and accompanied by a narrow brown, dry border. Damage is never so complete that it decimates a whole leaf as a caterpillar might. Typically, the weevil attacks primarily lower leaves because it's too much trouble to rise from the soil at sundown, travel to the top of the tree, and return to its hiding place in the soil

8-5

by sunrise. Caterpillars, however, often attack the succulent new growth at the top of the tree and roll up into a convenient leaf for a daytime nap. Raise your growing bench up on nails (8–5) and put the nails, hammered into the bench's legs, into small cans. Fill the small cans with water so that all crawling insects will no longer have access to your bonsai.

Granular insecticide, such as diazinon granules, makes a nice deterrent for this pest living in the soil. It is easily applied, like salt on an icy sidewalk. A light, even application is sufficient. A top layer of compost to cover the granules will make them more efficient. For persistent cases, an application of systemic insecticide may be necessary as with boring insects.

Gall Aphids

This last category of insects is perhaps among the most persistent pests known to bonsai. Fortunately, they are not common and tend to be limited to high-altitude conifers. These insects burrow into the newly forming buds of spruce, fir, hemlock, pine, and juniper. The infected bud tries to expand and grow, but it cannot because this parasite makes a nest inside it. I have tried to cut out the infected areas with a pruning tool and was disappointed the following year by resurgence of new infection sites. Apply systemic solution in late winter before bud growth begins. Three light applications two weeks apart are far more effective than one full-strength application. Protect bonsai roots from foliage runoff. After four hours, rinse the entire bonsai off with a gentle spray of clear water.

Remember, most insects are highly overrated as pests. Good observation and judicious application of common detergent will normally take care of the occasional problem. Second, there's much you can do to create a healthy environment for your trees. Water plants in the morning, remove standing water, and water only as needed. Encourage the presence of natural insect predators in your garden by cutting back on pesticides except when absolutely necessary. We can share the natural world with the praying mantis, ladybug, dragonfly, spider, lizard, and other natural helpful insects.

DISEASE

In the plant world *disease* refers to the natural process by which the cellulose of living tissues is recycled back into compost. In the case of bonsai, we obviously would like to slow down that process. We would prefer not to see our favorite pine tree bonsai turn into compost. Yet, this natural force is always present and at work in nature twenty-four hours a day. The task of the bonsai grower is to slow this process down so that we can enjoy watching our trees grow and develop. Without our interference, bonsai naturally wither, decline, rot, and return to the earth in the never-ending cycle of life.

Bonsai should be kept clean of falling leaves, seed casings, or other debris. Immediately prune off dead twigs, expired flower petals, and loose bark. Treat all driftwood areas with lime sulfur straight from the bottle.

The bark of a bonsai oak tree is shown in **8–6**. Since this is live bark and not an intentional dead area on a bonsai, we want to keep it clean, but not as bright as driftwood gray. We can accomplish this by applying a dilute mixture of lime sulfur instead of full strength. Use about 1 tablespoon per quart of water. Scrub the trunk with a toothbrush slightly moistened in this solution. The trunk will not turn its full gray color for forty-eight hours; so, don't judge the color immediately. If a lighter color is desired on your trunk, just reapply more of the solution. It keeps its strength for several weeks.

The bonsai bench should be made of cedar or redwood which naturally resists decay. Another alternative is to construct a bench surface of hardware cloth or soffit screen stretched across a lumber framework. Move the bonsai around often and wash off the bench under each pot once a week. Disease organisms hide there. Once a year, in summer, remove all your bonsai from the bench, and apply a strong bleach solution to the entire bench, its legs, cross supports, back, and especially the surface. Apply a solution of half water and half household bleach to your bench with a hand-pressurized insecticide sprayer. Scrub green scum away with a stiff brush. Leave the solution on for an hour, hose it off with fresh water, and return the bonsai to their places again. If you prefer the natural brown wood color rather then the bleached appearance, merely apply a wood preservative a week later. Allow the bleach time to work.

Try not to water the trunks of your trees, if possible. Although it's easier to spray water from a hose than to water with a watering can, constant moisture on tree bark creates scum. Lower the water pressure on your hose so that you can duplicate the stream of water that comes from the end of a bonsai watering can.

If algae begin to form on the surface of your pot, it's because your roots are too crowded, you've applied too much fertilizer, or you're watering too much. Sometimes all three problems exist. The solution is a firm blast from the garden hose and scrubbing with a toothbrush. A clean bonsai surface drains well.

Try to water in the morning rather than later in the day. You will be watering in the morning dew, before it has a chance to evaporate away, then adding sufficient additional moisture to last through the heat of the day. Avoid watering at night because bonsai take too long to dry off. Both insects and disease enjoy this prolonged wet condition. Slugs love it too. If your bonsai requires water twice a day, the second watering should occur about an hour before sundown. This gives the bonsai a chance to get its surfaces dry before nightfall. Wet foliage attracts fungus spores, since they stick to wet surfaces better than dry surfaces. Most common molds and mildews are caused by excess water or by watering at the wrong time of day, such as rust, powdery mildew, and black spot. Fungicides, of course, will treat these problems, but proper watering will prevent them.

A lesser-known disease is called *shot hole*, for obvious reasons. Most people would not recognize this as a fungus problem. The holes in the leaves make one think that an insect is responsible for the damage, but not so. This disease prefers elm, hornbeam, alder, birch, beech, and zelkova. Fungal spores in damp climates attach to the undersides of the leaves and rot away a small hole in the leaf (see **8–7**). The presence of small brownish half-rotted spots sometimes helps to

8–6

8–7

identify this problem as fungus rather than insect damage. The only success I have had, once the problem finds itself on my bonsai, is an application of powdered systemic fungicide, such as Benomyl, at dusk. Follow the application instructions on the product label.

EMERGENCY TREATMENT

Inspection

Bonsai can show many kinds of stress. Sometimes this stress comes from a single source. Other times, it may be due to a variety of insults. Observe your tree thoroughly from top to bottom. Look for subtle signs of stress. Examine the foliage. If it is damaged, where specifically is it damaged? What do the undersides of leaves look like? If wilted, is the root ball dry or wet? Is there a change in normal color for the plant? Are the woody branches affected in any way? Are portions of the trunk discolored or soft? Do surface roots seem slippery?

Gently pull the plant from the pot and inspect the root ball. Start by smelling the root mass. Does it smell like mushrooms or rotting vegetables? Is the soil completely or almost absent? Are the root hairs white and crisp? Do you see dark, slippery roots? Are fungus or mycorrhizae present? Examine the empty pot. Do you find any insects, excess calcified scale, or large cracks?

Be as thorough as you can with your inspection. Too often, wilting is seen as lack of water only; so, the bonsai is watered and ignored. But a wilted plant may be trying to communicate a more serious problem. Observe it carefully. Sometimes it's not just eyes but nose and fingers that uncover the problem. Manipulate the branches and the trunk carefully. You may discover an invisible mechanical break from a fall or from a squirrel. Squeeze and poke at the roots with a finger, and smell the freshly opened-up areas of soil for signs of root rot.

Spend several minutes going over every surface of your bonsai. Correct identification of a problem often combines two seemingly unrelated problems. Sometimes your plant has more than one problem.

When you are confident that you have carefully gone over every square inch of your bonsai, review the checklist for emergency care.

Checklist for Emergency Care

Observation	Possible Cause	Suggested Treatment
Wilted foliage, dry root ball	Not enough water	Soak bonsai root ball, pot and all, in a shallow tray, such as a kitty-litter box. Place in full shade and mist the foliage.
Persistent wilted foliage; dry root ball	Root-bound	Repot immediately. Spray foliage with an antidesiccant. Trim roots carefully and place the plant in a larger container if necessary.
Wilted foliage; wet root ball; smelly roots	Root rot	Remove plant from container and clean roots with the force of the hose nozzle. Trim away all dark, slippery roots. Immerse roots in a solution of systemic fungicide. Repot.

(continued)

Observation	Possible Cause	Suggested Treatment
Wilted foliage; wet root ball; white roots	Sucking insects	Place the bonsai where the root ball drains well and stays warm from the sun. Start alternately misting the foliage with clear water one day and mild detergent the next. Remove any visible insects with tweezers.
Wilted foliage; wet root ball; brown leaf edges	Sun scald	Move bonsai into shade. Trim off dead areas of leaves and branches. Lightly fertilize and wait for new growth to appear.
Wilted foliage; wet root ball; discolored leaves; twig dieback	Blight	Trim away all dead and stressed areas. Treat with a systemic fungicide. Sterilize your tools. Plant bonsai in the ground away from other similar plants.
Twig dieback; other foliage normal	Too cold last winter	Trim away damaged areas. Fertilize lightly and re-design bonsai to fill in healthy bare areas.
Sudden color change on one branch	Virus	Trim away affected areas and sterilize your tools.
Yellow leaves; green veins	Chlorosis	Fertilize with plenty of water before and after. Re-apply in one week.
Yellow leaves and veins	Mineral deficiency	Apply trace mineral fertilizer, including iron, sulfur, manganese, magnesium, and zinc.
Tiny holes in leaves	Shot-hole fungus	Apply systemic fungicide.
Leaves chewed away	Insect damage	See "Insects" section.
Top of tree is dying	Sunburn	Move bonsai to shade and mist foliage.
Bottom of tree is dying	Too much shade	Rotate your tree and prune away congested areas in the top of it. Fertilize lightly.
Pale color in conifer; dry root ball; tiny webs	Red spider mites	Apply Miticide or ten applications of detergent solution at three-day intervals. Prune away heavy foliage. Place in warm, sunny location.
Holes in dead wood	Borers	Inject any insecticide into holes with a syringe.
Constant oozing of sap from wound	Borers	Clean off wound with turpentine. Inject insecticide into any visible wound holes. Apply systemic insecticide to entire tree.
Scum on trunk	Overwatering	Scrub off scum with toothbrush. Water roots only, not trunk.
Scum on dead wood	Rot	Apply full-strength lime sulfur with small brush.
Scum on pot	Algae	Remove bonsai from pot. Soak pot in mild chlorine bleach solution; drain and scrub. Apply a light mineral oil to pot, then repot.
White crust on pot	Mineral, salt deposit	Remove bonsai from pot. Soak pot in vinegar solution overnight. Scrub with brush and rinse well. Apply light coat of mineral oil to pot, then repot.
White crust on soil surface	Mineral, salt deposit	Soak bonsai pot and roots in shallow tray for one half hour, rinse well. Water more deeply in the future.

Observation	Possible Cause	Suggested Treatment
Green scum on soil surface	Overwatering	Check to see if roots are too crowded. In the future, water this bonsai only when surface is dry.
Liverwort in pot	Too much nitrogen	When applying fertilizer, wash off excess with final rinse. Do not apply slow-release granules to soil surface.
Insects in soil	Drain holes are no longer covered	Clean out empty pot and reattach new soil screens with fresh copper staples. Sprinkle a few diazinon granules in bottom of pot, then repot.
Ants crawling all over bonsai	Aphids	Treat foliage with detergent as you would for aphids even if not visible. The ants are just an indicator of a sucking insect.
Red leaves on green plant	Heat exhaustion	Move plant to shadier location. Mist foliage; water well.
New buds fail to open	Phosphorus deficiency	Fertilize lightly with 0–10–10 and bone meal.
Flowers fail to open	Potassium deficiency	Fertilize as above.
Flowers fail to produce	No pollination	It might have been too cold for bees to do their work. If it is still not too late to fruit, irritate the remaining flowers with a small brush.
White powder on leaves	Mildew	Treat with systemic fungicide. Move bonsai to sunnier location. Water only in the morning. Trim away affected areas; sterilize tools.
Black spots on leaves	Fungus	Treat as above.
Rust-colored powder on leaves	Fungus	Treat as above. See "Disease" section.
Sudden large leaves	Excess nitrogen	Water your bonsai well to leach out excess fertilizer. Place in sunny location and trim off unsightly foliage.
Sudden foliage drop	Heat stroke	Move bonsai to shade, mist remaining foliage. Water well once, then water sparingly until recovery.
Leaves too small	Pot-bound	Repot.
Leaves too small	Not pot-bound; lack of nitrogen	Fertilize lightly.
White flecks on leaves	Scale	Touch fleck with a little mineral oil on a cotton applicator stick.
Flying dandruff	White fly	Apply insecticidal soap. See "Insects" section.
New growth wilted	Winter damage	Check roots. If they look healthy, move bonsai into shade and water sparingly.
Last year's growth falling off	Too hot	Move bonsai to shadier location. Water well once, then sparingly until foliage stops dropping. Apply vitamin B_1 solution to root ball after one week.
One suddenly dead branch	Mechanical damage	Look for a break in the branch. Perhaps a falling object hit it or a cat jumped on it. Check also for wire damage. Trim off branch.

(continued)

Observation	Possible Cause	Suggested Treatment
Large hole in soil	Squirrel or large bird	It may be necessary to wrap the bonsai with protective screen. Avoid feeding these animals with nuts and berries if possible. Sometimes a toy pinwheel will keep these animals at a distance.
Long, leggy growth	Not enough light	Move the tree to a sunnier location. Trim off unsightly growth. Pinch back new shoots often.
Blue conifer fading to green	Magnesium deficiency	Apply a pinch of Epsom salts to your liquid fertilizer. Blue color intensifies in sunny location. Make sure to give it enough light. Existing growth is difficult to change.
No flowers on tree	Incorrect pruning	If your tree is four years old or more, flowers will form each year. Heavy annual pruning usually removes flower spurs. Prune only after flowers fade for best results.

If you're still not sure what to do, pull the bonsai out of its pot and place it on the bonsai shelf without its pot. With a moderate stream of water, rinse the foliage, branches, trunk, and roots with clear water. While it is still dripping wet, place the root ball on the ground in your garden where you know the soil is free of pesticides. Do not dig a hole for the roots. Mound plenty of fresh compost over the root ball and water it in thoroughly. Set a sprinkler nearby and, for the next three days, make sure the tree is watered well. After one week, apply a light application of systemic insecticide and systemic fungicide together. (Products, such as Orthenex, combine them for you.) Wait ten days and apply again. After two weeks, apply a light liquid fertilizer. Grow this bonsai as a small shrub for as long as it takes to show healthy foliage and vigorous growth again. It might take one or two years. You can always repot it later. The important thing is that you've saved the tree. After all, you want to keep your bonsai alive.

9

SEASONAL
CHECKLIST

Here's a checklist of seasonal activities you should be engaged with whether you cultivate a single bonsai or many. The timing of "early winter," "late spring," and other seasonal divisions will of course depend on your regional climate. These divisions may equal a month in one region but be shorter or longer in another.

EARLY WINTER

Prune fall-blooming bonsai. This includes some magnolia, chrysanthemum, camellia, or similar plants. Since new buds are formed in late spring, do your severe pruning for shape now to avoid harvesting next year's blossoms during spring pruning.

Pay careful attention to watering. Remember, one complete, useful watering consists of three consecutive waterings, even in winter. Light watering or incomplete watering only promotes mineral buildup in the container. If you water, then water thoroughly or not at all. But be careful. Bonsai foliage often forms a natural canopy over the pot, and even in a downpour of rain the pot won't be watered sufficiently. Take advantage of this natural moisture and humidity. Water in anticipation of a great downpour of rain and your bonsai will appreciate it.

Clean pots of mineral residues. Pull the bonsai from the container and wrap the root ball in a wet, saturated towel. Soak the empty pot in a shallow container of water and vinegar; then scrub it with a stiff brush. Alternately soak and brush the pot until clean. Apply a light coat of mineral oil to the outside of the pot to restore the original patina; then repot. For problem containers, it may be necessary to pot your tree in a temporary container. You can then plant the calcified bonsai pot deep in the ground for a year. Soil bacteria and microorganisms will clean the pot thoroughly for you. Just remember where you buried it.

Apply lime sulfur to deciduous trees. The simple application of a dormant spray is always underrated. It is difficult to overemphasize the importance of this application. When winter comes, the bugs are not around anymore; so, the lax bonsai grower supposes insect and disease problems are gone until next year. This is like the man who doesn't fix his roof because it's not raining. The early-winter season is ideal for a preventive application of lime sulfur to deciduous trees. Lime sulfur is a wonderful pesticide (as well as fungicide) that's made of lime and sulfur, not chlorinated hydro-

carbons which pollute ground water and cause problems in the food chain. Apply it now and enjoy success later next year. Ignore this time and suffer the myriad problems coming your way in spring. Simply follow directions on the label. Do not allow it to drip into the bonsai container.

Use no fertilizer. As with late fall, no additional nutrition is needed for your plants. What nutrient the bonsai needs has already been stored in the plant tissues of stems and roots. In addition, fertilizer delivered to the plant at this time would be wasted because of low ambient temperature and the bonsai's lack of growth activity.

Water early in the day. Overnight temperatures drop suddenly at dusk. This creates a real problem both for bonsai and their pots. When water turns suddenly into ice crystals, a brief period of rapid expansion occurs. Water in a closed container, such as a cascade pot, expands quickly as the temperature decreases from 32° F to 31° F. This force is powerful enough to explode bonsai pots. Similarly, excess water in your bonsai plant's vascular tissues at dusk can do irreparable harm to the natural veins that carry water and nutrition throughout the plant. Succulent white root tips are most susceptible to this exploding phenomenon during freezing. Early watering in the day provides bonsai the time to rid itself of excess moisture before dusk. This additional times allows tiny air spaces to be incorporated between soil particles. Also, minerals and starches have time to accumulate in vascular tissues of the plant again. This helps protect the plant from freezing just as though you added antifreeze to its pipes.

Remove large clumps of moss. Excess moss in winter harbors insects and disease. Excess moss holds moisture in the pot at a dangerously high level. Removing this excess vegetation improves soil drainage, increases beneficial oxygen to the roots, and warms the root ball by allowing the winter sun to contact the soil and container.

Do not transplant trees. Repotting is a traumatic event in the life of a plant. In winter, broken root hairs do not have the ability to repair themselves because they are not growing. The tree's natural immune system is low. Bacteria and fungus can successfully invade the plant. Root rot occurs as spring approaches. It's better to let the bonsai rest without damage. Be patient; wait until spring.

Collect rocks. Rocks for rock plantings, landscapes, viewing stones, and saikei. Look for the perfect rock to place under the exposed roots of a juniper or maple you've been growing. Make plans for a root-over-rock planting, utilizing a young seedling you're developing.

Disinfect your bonsai bench. Remove all trees to a safe distance and apply a solution of half water and half household bleach to all surfaces. I find that a compressed-air sprayer does a fine job. The strong bleach solution will spot your clothes and damage adjacent plants; so, be careful during application. Scrub unusually slippery green or dark areas with a brush. Where water tends to stand, either tilt the bench or drill holes in it to improve drainage. After letting this solution stand for one hour, spray it all clean with a good hard blast with fresh water from your garden hose. Wait one week before applying oil preservatives; the bleach will continue to work.

Finish cleaning up fall debris. Pick up all leaves and needles from around your miniature bonsai. Pluck off any remaining leaves that continue to cling to their branches. Wipe off the bottoms of all your pots. Move your bonsai to different locations on the bench to avoid discoloring one particular spot. Especially clean up your yard. Remove all debris that will decompose in the winter. Falling twigs and branches from overhanging or adjacent trees harbor the insects and disease that can attack your trees this coming spring. Thorough mulching is one solution; complete removal of these hosts is another solution. It just depends on your circumstances.

Sketch your trees. Bring your bonsai into your home, one at a time. Put them on your best display stand and contemplate them for a while. You may not be a proficient pen-and-ink artist, but denying that you have artistic skill means that you cannot design bonsai. Make two drawings of each tree. The first drawing should be what you'd like this bonsai to look like next winter. The next drawing should be what you'd like it to look like in ten years. Save these drawings and look at them again next winter. Did you accomplish your goals? If not, then do you know why? What are you going to do this year that you did not do last year? Are you letting the tree design itself or are you in control?

Wire deciduous bonsai. After your maple or elm tree has been inside the house for a couple of days, it becomes dry and needs to be taken back outside and watered well. But before you do, this is a good time to wire and bend the branches. Wilted celery in the neglected corner of your refrigerator vegetable compartment is flaccid and flexible. It can be easily bent without breaking. The branches of deciduous trees are similar. When fresh and loaded with nutrition and water, they're crisp and break easily. After a few days in the house, the branches on a deciduous tree become fairly supple and pliable. They're partially wilted. So, you can wind them with copper wire and bend them into appropriate conformations without splitting or cracking. The next day, you can lightly water the bonsai so that branches slowly return to their normal turgor. Do *not* water heavily immediately after wiring. Let the branches adjust slowly to their new positions.

Read books, take notes, and make plans for the future. Take advantage of the relatively slow time in your annual bonsai calendar to catch up on tasks you normally place on the back burner. Use this quiet time to do important developmental tasks. This is also a good time to observe others' bonsai.

MIDWINTER

Enjoy the indoor display of your bonsai. Nothing is quite as satisfying as a fine, twiggy deciduous bonsai to greet you in the living room or a shapely pine tree welcoming holiday guests as they arrive. Group miniatures together for best display.

Bare-root broadleaf evergreens, if necessary. One of the disadvantages of growing camellias, rhododendrons, azaleas, and similar plants as bonsai is that the broad evergreen leaf surfaces make them less dormant and seasonally periodic than other plants. Green leaves present year-round capture the sun's rays even in winter. They are highly successful plants as a group. Just look around you in the winter and note the huge number of varieties and shapes available. Some are trees but most are shrubs and hedges. A few ground covers even make good bonsai if trained for a few years up on a stake. In midwinter you can drastically dig into their root balls. Avoid cutting roots if possible. Alternate a strong water flow with combing action from a dull root rake or chopsticks for best results. This drastic action would be harmful any other time of year.

Begin cold stratification of seed. Most outdoor bonsai species require a period of moist cold before sowing. Place your seed in a large kettle of warm water overnight. Crack open the shells of hard, coated seeds the next morning. Place the seed in several moist handfuls of coarse sphagnum moss that has been lightly sprinkled with fungicide. Place the moss and seeds together in a plastic bag and store them for the remainder of winter in the coldest part of your refrigerator. You don't need to freeze them. In early spring, wash and clean the seeds and sow them in a coarse planting mix in a protected area, such as a windowsill or greenhouse. Transplant when the roots are 3 inches long.

Remove mistletoe. Having mistletoe on your oak tree may be fascinating, but it's a parasite. It will weaken your bonsai. Physical removal may not be effective the first time, but persistent removal will eliminate the problem. Many high-altitude conifers collected from nature may also have this pest. Carefully check native materials in their first few years in your garden. Avoid the spread of insects and disease. Even quarantine them if necessary.

Don't use fertilizer in midwinter. Check your soil carefully and examine its health. Watch for signs of alkali buildup, calcium residues, or salt. If you live in an area with hard water, it would be a good idea to add soil sulfur or Miracid to your bonsai soil at this time every year. If your water is soft, check for green slime, abundant moss, liverwort, and signs of acid soil or nitrogen buildup. Correct these soils with bone meal, agricultural limestone, or wood ash. The plant's performance this coming year will be noticeably better if you do.

Water protected bonsai. Don't forget the plants protected under your benches, next to the house, or buried in a cold frame. It's easy to neglect them—out of sight, out of mind. On warm, windy days, they'll appreciate an extra dose of moisture. Avoid watering after noon.

Check your stock of bonsai soil. Spring is coming soon. In late winter bare-rooting season begins and those plants use up a lot of soil. Screen more if necessary. Do not run out in the middle of your busiest transplanting season.

Double check your preparation for a sudden cold snap. It's frustrating to sit down for a warm evening meal and hear the pop of a cascade pot outside or the first stones of a hailstorm. Watch the weather reports regularly and have backup systems for your emergency equipment. Keep plenty of spare light bulbs, flashlight batteries, extra extension cords, and plastic sheeting. Since you may have to move your plants indoors into a garage or utility room suddenly, make sure the area is clean and ready. Keep a few small folding tables or benches handy to make it convenient. In the event of a power outage, are your greenhouse plants safe or would you lose the whole crop? A portable generator or propane heater might be a good investment.

Make the first application of copper. Some growers prefer the use of lime sulfur as a dormant spray, others prefer a copper-based liquid. I think both are equally effective; however, copper used throughout winter, beginning just after leaf drop in the fall, causes a little trunk and branch discoloration, particularly in irregular or corky barks. In addition, the nice creamy white of zelkova, elm, or birch can be darkened with repeated applications. If you restrict copper applications to midwinter or late winter only, this problem is not noticeable.

Plan for spring growth and list the tasks ahead. Which tree must be bare-rooted? Which trees need transplanting? Which need to be transplanted from the

Do not risk damage to flowers by applying these dormant sprays too late. If winter bulbs are sprouting from the ground, stop any further dormant spray applications. Ideally, you should have had time for four applications from last fall until now.

Consider gall aphid control. Late winter is the only time of the year when the gall aphid actively seeks a new home in your fir, pine, spruce, or hemlock. If your tree has the characteristic signs of this pest, several judicious applications of insecticidal soap will take care of the gall aphid now. If you miss this opportunity, you'll have to use a systemic insecticide because the insect is well hidden and protected inside the tree for the rest of the year.

Train conifers now. The sap in conifers is just starting to flow slowly. They have not built up enough turgor pressure yet to expand their buds, however. So that makes this an ideal time to bend, twist, or shape large branches or trunks. As usual, withhold water for several days, wrap the branch or trunk with raffia or floral tape for protection; then bend gradually with wire, clamps, or turnbuckles. You can accomplish astonishing results at this time that would be impossible later in the year.

Prune early-blooming deciduous trees. Soon the flowers will open up. If you prune now, you can not only prune for shape, but you can prune knowing where the flowers are going to be. There's already a difference in the size and shape between fruiting and vegetative buds; so, you can determine how many flowers you'll allow to bloom. A miniature bonsai needs only a few flowers to look its best.

Use the first fertilizer of the year. Apply a light application of liquid 10–15–10 or similar fertilizer. Add a few drops of the liquid to a watering can full of water that has been standing a few hours. Apply this solution slowly to the moist bonsai root ball. Wait thirty minutes; then rinse your bonsai with fresh water.

Bare-root conifers. This is an excellent time to transfer conifers from the ground into their first containers. Severe root pruning is acceptable now. As always, trim away a little foliage to compensate for the lack of roots.

Beware of unusual warm weather. Check all your trees daily, especially your miniature bonsai. After a little sunny or windy weather, some pots will need moisture, others will not. Do not water a moist bonsai.

ground into their first bonsai pot? Which trees will be grafted? Which need drastic restyling? Prioritize your list so that you'll complete the most important projects in timely fashion.

Sharpen your tools. Since this season is the least busy, it's an excellent chance to catch up on this often neglected aspect of bonsai training. Have a professional sharpen them if you feel uncomfortable doing it yourself. Remember when you made the first smooth cut with your brand-new bonsai shears? And now why be willing to tolerate blisters and risk carpal tunnel syndrome from dull, rusty tools. Restore that just-new feeling.

LATE WINTER

Make the last application of dormant spray. Unseasonably warm days may cause quick swelling of tight buds on early-blooming deciduous trees, like quince.

Prepare beds for cuttings. As buds begin to swell, suddenly it will become perfect weather for taking cuttings. Prepare garden beds by mounding fresh soil into a raised row or between two large timbers. Increased drainage and air circulation favor the delicate new cuttings. If you prefer, you can use portable trays or boxes which can be moved about as the temperature fluctuates. This latter method is good if field mice, squirrels, or large aggressive birds are around. A screen mesh of hardware cloth can be nailed to the top of your cutting box to discourage pests.

Graft in late winter. Sap moves slightly, but so slowly that it doesn't interfere with the union of the scion to the stock plant. Check more specialized texts for the many ways to graft. Whatever method you choose, the cambium layers of both the scion and the host plant must *precisely* meet each other and the cuts must be freshly made with an extremely sharp knife. Otherwise, the graft will not work. Sealing the cut area will protect the graft until the callus forms and the wound heals itself naturally.

EARLY SPRING

Prune early-blooming deciduous azaleas and rhododendrons. The popular Exbury and Mollus azaleas provide spectacular flowers this month. Actually, quite a number of early-blooming shrubs are nice for miniature bonsai, including forsythia, star magnolia, witch hazel, sasanqua camellia, quince, and wild cherry. As soon as the blooms fade, severe pruning back of the bonsai will restore their shape and still not harvest next year's blooms. For two more months, pinch back new vegetative growth as it appears, then stop.

Shape deciduous trees as they sprout. Once your basic tree outline is formed, maintain it by pinching new growth back regularly throughout the growing season. Next year, you will be rewarded with a fine twiggy tree. Wire as necessary before the new growth completely obscures your efforts.

Check your wires from last year. If they will not accommodate this year's spring expansion, it is better to replace them now, while you can still see the branches. Test wire clearance. You should be able to poke a wire between the branch and the training wire around it. If not, it's better to replace it now while you can.

Bare-root azaleas this month. The technical term for this process isn't quite *bare-root*, but we lack a better term. Nursery azaleas, potted for landscaping purposes, are planted in a soil mix that's mostly peat moss. Peat is appropriate for landscaping since the plants are transplanted in the ground. This soil is short-lived for bonsai, however. If you're developing a bonsai azalea in a pot, this is a time to comb out as much peat as you can without disturbing the azalea's roots. You'll probably tear some roots in the process. Just don't tear too many at one time. You may have to finish the job next year. Try to incorporate as much coarse bonsai soil as you can between the roots at this time. The pot will drain better, and your azalea will develop roots that resemble those of a conifer rather than the typical spongy amorphous roots found growing in peat.

Plant root-over-rock projects. Comb out the roots of a 3- to 5-year-old plant and place them around a shapely, interesting rock. Lightly bind the roots with floral tape or wide rubber bands. Plant the roots, rock and all, into the ground or a large container. Grow for one more year. Then gradually start brushing away the soil from the top of the rock. You will be well on your way to a stunning root-over-rock planting in just two years. Other methods are tedious and less effective.

Thread graft in early spring. (See chapter 7 for details.) The terminal buds on conifers and deciduous trees are swelling and committed. Drill a hole completely through the trunk as small as you can without damaging this bud. Secure the graft with a straight pin on the opposite side and wait. For pine, this graft takes two years, but maple will be ready by fall.

Bring trees out of winter protection. Trees that have been stored in greenhouses will burn when first exposed to direct sun. Allow this transition to happen gradually. Deciduous trees that break their dormancy can be pruned back lightly and allowed to get used to the sunshine again. Do not prune off all spindly growth at one time. Eventually, however, it will all have to come off. Open the cold frame a little longer every day, especially in the morning when the sun first starts to heat up the enclosed space. Transplant ground-planted bonsai as soon as their buds start to show activity. Do not wait for new growth to appear since that will be too late.

Adjust to unseasonably hot or cold weather. For hot weather, protect tender growth from sunburn. Water well and do not fertilize. For unusual cold snaps, move plants back into your cold frame, garage, or unheated

utility room. Withhold water and mound plenty of mulch over the soil surfaces. A little fertilizer added to the mulch will actually help heat the root ball.

Control growth by intentional wilting. As new growth emerges strong and upright, cut back on watering slightly until you see the first signs of wilting. Then water sparingly. If you repeat this process several times a week in early spring, your new growth will appear smaller, stronger, and more compact. Unlimited water in the spring, by contrast, encourages large, long, upright, and fragile growth that's best pruned away. Try this technique whenever you can in early spring, but you need to be extra careful with smaller pots, or overwilting will cause damage.

Set blossoms by hand if necessary. Sometimes when it's warm and too rainy for bees, pollination becomes spotty, and fruit does not follow the flower. If these conditions exist when your fruiting bonsai comes into bloom, irritate the inside of each flower with a small artist's brush, allowing pollination without bees, and your fruit will be set.

Give your bonsai a good dose of fertilizer at least twice in early spring. Water well, then apply diluted 5–10–10 or a similar formula. Wait thirty minutes and water well again.

Trim off water sprouts as they appear. After severe pruning on a fruit tree, strong vertical shoots appear later. These shoots are sometimes called water sprouts because they appear after spring rains begin. Actually, they're just new branches that are growing too fast to develop strength. They always appear after heavy pruning. The tree attempts to quickly restore the balance between root and foliage growth. Immediately remove buds that appear where they're not needed, such as along the tops of branches. Thin out large clumps of buds that appear around a pruning scar. Retain only one or two buds. As new growth extends itself, prune it back to only one or two leaves. Prune so that you point the terminal leaf in the direction you desire further growth.

Transplant in early spring. This is the easiest and most practical time to do major potting, repotting, styling, bending, and pruning. A month later will be inappropriate to do drastic work on plants. Get accustomed to working earlier in the year. Your plants will appreciate it.

Make deciduous cuttings of stone fruits and flowering trees. Prepare your cutting beds prior to taking cuttings. The secret to success is threefold. First, *tear* off your cuttings rather than cut them off with a sharp scissors. This helps concentrate natural healing and growth hormones. Second, application of rooting hormone and the cutting itself must happen in a matter of seconds, not minutes. For this reason, a portable tray filled with sand or perlite brought to the donor tree is useful. If you prefer growing cuttings in the ground, either make the cutting bed right nearby, or bring the host tree over to the cutting bed and make your cuttings there. Third, the soil must drain perfectly so that you can lightly mist the fresh cuttings at will without danger of excess dampness.

Evaluate each of your trees. We often put off projects we should be doing. But we'll accept advice from others concerning our own trees, while being lazy about our

own plans. Look at your trees in early spring with a cold, unforgiving eye. Sometimes it helps to look at a photograph of your tree. If it's too tall, it doesn't take a rocket scientist to figure out what to do. Just do it. This is the best time.

MIDSPRING

Take cuttings from conifers. Place these cuttings into pure sand or perlite; soil does not drain well enough. Your cuttings will rot before they root. I find that liquid-rooting hormone works better than powder for conifers, and that a bit of DMSO (dimethyl sulphoxide) added to the hormone will drive it into the tough plant tissues faster. Remember, with cuttings, speed is important. Do not ever combine DMSO with a pesticide, because this combination is extremely toxic.

Prune early-blooming bonsai. By now, your flowering cherry, apple, plum, camellia, and many other plants have bloomed. Trim back for general shape and thin out branches before the vegetative growth gets heavy. Where the sun doesn't shine, leaves will die.

Twist off long pine candles. The presence of pine candles this early indicates strong hormonal growth. Removal of the strongest and longest candles this early will help redistribute growth throughout the plant. Remember that growth hormones work in reverse. That is, removal of strong growth means that you're physically taking away a bud-inhibitor hormone that encourages side shoots and small internodes. Remove the most powerful candles entirely. Do not make the mistake of retaining any part of the candle; growth will only be redirected to the fragment that remains.

Begin pinching back new growth. A compact bud contains all the blueprints for a very long branch. It is your task to make sure it doesn't extend to this length. Here's a good rule of thumb during growing season. Allow three leaves or three pairs of leaves to emerge from a developing bud, then pinch back to one leaf or one pair of leaves. With conifers, simply shape the new growth as it appears. Nip off the new growth while it is chartreuse and succulent. If you need to use a pruning tool, you've waited too long.

Control slugs and snails. Wet spring weather will hatch thousands of new gastropods. Buy an inexpensive brand of beer, and leave a few shallow containers of it lying around the growing area.

Water rapidly growing bonsai only. The first signs of plant distress are that the root balls do not take up moisture in the spring. If you broadcast water randomly or universally over your collection, you cannot notice their distress call. Plants that remain wet in spring need to be treated with a fungicide and be planted in the ground.

Begin to rotate your plants. Turn them around on the bench. Let all sides enjoy the sunshine. They will develop in a more balanced and even fashion.

Wire weak branches upward. If you are having trouble developing a lower branch, wire it up instead of down. Place this weak branch toward the sun, which helps redistribute balance of growth on your bonsai.

Move your plants around to regulate growth. A maple that's producing leggy growth needs more sun, a sulking juniper needs more sun, and a sunburned elm needs to be pruned back and placed in a shadier location. You can regulate water, growth, and direction of development this month by moving your plants around, depending on their individual needs. As the weather becomes warmer, miniature bonsai will require afternoon shade.

Transplant pine, fir, hemlock, and spruce. Do not bare-root, but transfer the root ball carefully from one container to another. Remove mud, silt, debris, and decaying organic matter. Rinse the root ball several times with a moderate stream of fresh water while the roots are out of the pot. Pine roots often have a symbiotic association, called mycorrhiza, with the mycelium of a fungus. Always retain a little of whitish fungus and transplant some along with the roots. The relationship between fungus and roots is well documented in pine, but it occurs in other seed plants as well. We're just now beginning to appreciate the importance of soil microorganisms. Retain a little soil mold when transplanting all trees, since it seems beneficial.

Watch for aphids. New succulent growth in midspring attracts many kinds of sucking insects, including the ubiquitous aphids. Observe this new growth carefully and apply insecticidal soap immediately for quick and easy results. Once the colony grows, the task becomes far more difficult.

LATE SPRING

Take cuttings of *kurume* and *satsuki* azaleas. If your cutting has a flower remnant on it or a lingering seed pod, pinch it out carefully. Always take more cuttings than you need, for they will not all sprout. You should get at least 60 percent of your cuttings to root successfully in a month. Transplant when the roots are at least 1½ inches long, which will take about eight weeks.

Prune maples often. Wait until the third pair of leaves just begin to emerge from the new shoot, then prune back to only one pair. To avoid scarring, remove unwanted new buds from the trunk as they become visible.

Wilt conifers occasionally. New growth should not always come out strong and full of moisture. Withhold water until new shoots just start to droop; then mist the foliage. Water deeply the following morning. The process will strengthen new growth, make it shorter, and decrease the size of the internodes.

Check the drain holes on your pots. Pick up the pots and examine them carefully to see if the root mass is pulling the screens away from the drain holes, allowing insects easy access to the soil. Quick repotting may be necessary. Trim excess rootage away from the holes because it interferes with drainage. Look for signs of insects hiding under each pot. A light sprinkling of diazinon granules on the bench under the pots will discourage crawling pests.

Twist candles on pine. There are many ways to control the growth of pine. The most common method involves twisting off the majority of the longest candles and half of the medium-sized candles, and leaving the smallest ones alone.

Check wired branches. Spring is almost over, but most wires should remain one more month. If the wires start to cut into the bark, they must be cut off. Do not twist off the wire. You risk the chance of severely tearing the bark. Use wire cutters, even on the smaller gauges of wire utilized on miniature bonsai.

Repot late-blooming plants. Although they're few, there are bonsai that bloom in summer. This is their

springtime; so, it is safe to transplant them now without damage.

Tip cascading plants on their sides. Many cascading plants, like chrysanthemum, are hard to grow otherwise. Strong upward growth in a species usually means that lower branches tend to grow weak over time. This is a good time to invigorate these lower branches by tilting the bonsai so that the lowest branches are more upright and face the sun. It's even possible to grow bonsai upside down.

Prune according to visible vigor. Pinch back strong shoots hard, and rotate weak shoots toward the sun and prune them back only lightly. Especially prune away unwanted growth that shades important branches.

Watch for excess moisture during hot weather. This is the beginning of the mildew season. Fresh, succulent, warm, and wet growth are the first to get these diseases. Water only in the mornings, especially if you know it will be warm that day. Water all your bonsai well when it rains. Take advantage of the natural moisture they receive and drench them thoroughly with additional water. Foliage tends to act like an umbrella over the pot. You think they are getting really wet, but they're not. As a test, place a small can on the soil surface under the canopy of a bonsai. Compare moisture in this can with a similar can out in the open. You'll be surprised at the difference between the water levels in the two cans.

Start training tender new growth immediately. If you wait until midsummer to train your new maple branches, they'll be brittle and break off easily. If you wait until next year to train them, you'll get a rather weeping appearance near the trunk. You will no longer be able to get that nice, precise downward angle found on old specimens. Instead, carefully loop a wire around the new growth this month, and gently tease the young branch down into place by fastening the other end of the wire to the pot, a root, or even the bench itself. This type of wiring is the gentlest method. If you tie down a branch to the bench, don't forget that it's tied there when you rotate your tree.

EARLY SUMMER

This is your first opportunity to treat *jin*, *shari*, and *saba-miki*. In early summer, the average temperature will rise enough that the lime sulfur will be able to soak into the driftwood areas of your bonsai. In cooler weather, the lime sulfur concentrate tends to just coat these surfaces, and so it looks more like white paint than sun-bleached driftwood gray. Pour a small quantity of the concentrate, without diluting it, into a small glass container. Dip a small artist's brush in the liquid, and carefully paint all dead areas on your tree. After forty-eight hours the dead wood will be silvery gray and well preserved for another season. Apply additional coats as needed.

Select second-growth candles on your pine. By now, earlier pinching and twisting of the first candles will have forced new growth to begin. Rub out unwanted buds as soon as you can, without damaging adjacent desirable growth. Use tweezers if necessary, because fingers can be large and clumsy in cramped circumstances.

Pinch back growth on high-altitude conifers. For a few years after collection, these trees will break their buds at nearly the same time they would in the woods. These later-growing conifers will gradually adjust to lower elevations. For the first few years, however, give them the extra time to extend their new growth. Do not pinch them back in spring, but wait until early summer.

Leaf-trim deciduous trees. The first time I saw someone do this to a maple, I was skeptical, but it really works, especially on miniature bonsai. Just make sure you're doing it for the right reasons. The tree should be healthy, bonsai styling should be 90 percent or more complete, the leaves must be on a young, vigorously growing tree, and the leaves must be too large. If any of these conditions do not exist, standard pruning is best. Remember to use very sharp scissors and cut halfway between each leaf bud and its branch attachment. The remaining leaf stem should be allowed to fall off by itself. Carefully monitor water uptake for the first few weeks after defoliation. The tree cannot use water as rapidly without its leaves. Continued watering under this condition will cause root rot. In a few weeks, you will get tiny, perfectly shaped leaves that will give you a spectacular fall display.

Prune rhododendrons and azaleas. Any spring-blooming bonsai can be pruned back safely at this time. There are still enough long days left in the year so that the plant can reset new flower buds for next spring.

Pinch back oak. The first strong shoots of oak should appear now. To avoid excess elongation and large leaf size, pinch these strong shoots back to only one leaf. Secondary shoots will appear smaller and two of their leaves may be kept. Judge the severity of pruning necessary by observing leaf size. Retain small leaves. Heavily trim shoots that produce large leaves.

Thread-graft this month just as you would in spring. Pull off all the foliage that's in the way, even on conifers. Save an intact terminal bud and push the branch through the hole and secure it as you would in spring. New growth will arrive quickly.

Avoid watering at midday. This is the beginning of the summer season when the combination of moisture and heat can cause sun scald and mildew. Water early in the day. If an additional watering is needed, wait until after 4 P.M., but not as late as dusk. On a really dry day, water everything whether it needs it or not. Broadcast a large, fine stream of water over the foliage, branches, bench, and pots and under the benches and nearby structures,

too. The additional humidity and coolness will linger around your half-baked plants longer. Do not do this every day.

Watch for borers, thrips, and mites. Warm weather will bring out all kinds of insects. Check all your trees as you water each day. Do not let a week go by with these insects loose since they multiply quickly.

Transplant trees only on rainy days. If emergency repotting must be done, wait for an unusually cool or overcast day. If it doesn't arrive, then transplant indoors and leave the plant inside until an overcast day comes before moving it out. Protect recent plantings under the full shade of a tree.

Remember to train by intentional wilting. (See "Late Spring" section.)

Air-layer trees this month. Cut a wide swath that completely circles the trunk. Make your cut deep, beyond the cambium layer. Wrap with premoistened sphagnum moss. Then wrap first with clear plastic, and finally, black plastic. With this method, you can open the black plastic and check for white roots visible against the clear plastic.

Select fruit for display. By now the blossoms on your fruiting bonsai have faded and the fruit is starting to expand as it grows seeds, protective pulp, and skin. There's no point in keeping a hundred tiny kumquats on your citrus tree. Too much fruit will endanger the health of the bonsai. Prune away unneeded fruit. A good bonsai display will have only about fifteen fruits on a 20-inch tree. A tiny 6-inch miniature bonsai needs only five fruits to offer a stunning display.

MIDSUMMER

Remove large amounts of copper wire. Copper wire conducts heat extremely well. That's why good cookware is coated with copper. Unfortunately, this property turns copper wire into a liability in the hottest summer months. To the detriment of bonsai branches, copper passes the sun's heat along these coils. Aluminum also makes good cookware and bonsai wire. If you have a tree trained heavily with wire, remove most of it during the summer. Moving the tree into the shade will reduce the excess heat, but it will elongate new growth. It's better to remove the wire.

Treat *jin*, *shari*, and *saba-miki* this month with lime sulfur. Heat will help the chemical penetrate the dead wood.

Remove third-year growth on conifers. At this time of the year, needles three years old will naturally start to yellow and fall off. If you rip these needles away, you will stimulate the formation of new buds for next year. Conifer buds form where sunlight touches the branches, particularly where injury has occurred. By tearing off these old needles now, you can help stimulate a tremendous crop of new buds for next fall.

Remember to rotate your trees. Your trees will perform considerably better if you do this on a regular basis.

Watch for signs of heat stress. Excess heat can cause burned leaf margins, unusually small new leaves, wilt, and scorched leaf surfaces. Keep a careful eye for these signs. Miniature bonsai will enjoy a few days' vacation in the shade.

Fertilize this month with fish emulsion. The trace minerals in this organic slurry will benefit heat-stressed plants. As usual, apply the fertilizer with plenty of water before and after each application. Fertilize only on cloudy, overcast days.

Midsummer is the last period to defoliate. If you trim deciduous leaves completely off any later, you might not have enough warm days left to replace them with new growth. In warmer climates that risk is less.

Prune flowering and fruiting trees with respect for next year's bloom. Learn how to identify the different growth characteristics between flowering and vegetative growth. Each species is slightly different. Judicious pruning at this time will keep you from limiting your blossoms next spring. In general, prune for compact growth and close internodes. The bonsai's outside shape must be maintained. Limit the inside growth to enable strong branches to receive sunlight. Any other inside pruning or thinning may remove next year's fruit and flowers.

LATE SUMMER

Control secondary growth of maples. Most deciduous trees experience a short summer dormancy period in which new growth is temporarily arrested. In unseasonably cool summer days or during rainy weather, these trees will react as if spring has arrived again. Trim these new shoots just as you would in spring.

Water often and water deeply. Use a sprinkler, if necessary, to broadcast a lot of moisture around your bonsai, especially miniatures. As always, avoid midday moisture.

Apply 5–10–10 fertilizer, trace elements, and Epsom salts. Since fall is coming, these nutrients must be in the soil in advance to allow the tree to store valuable minerals and carbohydrates for the colder season. Three small applications in late summer are much better than one large dose.

Scrub the trunks with a toothbrush dipped in a dilute solution of lime sulfur. This cleaning will prevent and remove algae from bonsai like elm, birch, and zelkova that are getting lots of water.

Protect trees from afternoon sun. There is no special award given for the ability to grow a bonsai juniper in full sun where it is 100° F. When the temperature is this hot, shade your trees from 1 to 4 P.M. Watch the local weather report for unusually hot days. If you go on vacation, make sure your neighbor or alternate caregiver is aware of this potential problem.

Let your bonsai enjoy the remainder of the summer. Give them plenty of water and rest from constant sun. Fertilize sparingly, trim only when necessary, rotate often, wire with caution, and remove yellowing needles and leaves as they appear. Repot only in an emergency.

Prune to avoid dieback. Pretend your eyes are the sun and look over your trees from top to bottom. Rotate the trees on a turntable. If you cannot see through large clumpy areas of growth, trim these areas back to maintain the health of your bonsai. Otherwise, shaded areas

Plant root-over-rock bonsai, rock plantings, and saikei. Fall is a time of limited foliage growth and the beginning of a prolonged period of root growth. Take advantage of this season to create complex plantings that would be difficult in spring. In spring, stored root energy is ready to be expressed as foliage growth. When creating rock plantings, the primary goal is to establish the root mass, and this is the appropriate time.

Make the last application of fertilizer that contains nitrogen. With all nutrients we try to anticipate growth. Since we don't anticipate significant growth in midfall, we don't apply nitrogen after early fall. We can, however, anticipate continued formation of next year's buds and fall root growth. So the best fertilizer is 3–10–5 or something similar.

For better fall color, restrict water on deciduous trees. Once the leaves on a maple or elm turn color, they are essentially dormant. Sugars and minerals take over the job of maintaining these deciduous trees. Fall color in Vermont is spectacular, partly because of the lack of heavy rain in early fall. However, native fall color in Oregon, where I live, is limited to a few days, because autumn rains turn everything brown. But my bonsai retain their brilliant color longer due to my intentional limitation of water.

Water selectively. Like spring, fall produces conditions which favor some plants and not others. Actively growing conifers use moisture at a rate much greater than deciduous trees just going into dormancy. Water these two types of bonsai differently. Do not overwater or underwater.

Transplant deciduous trees. One distinct advantage of fall color is that it indicates when it is safe to repot. if the tree shows any color at all, it's safe to transplant. Take advantage of this opportunity to repot; it won't happen again until early spring.

This is an excellent time to collect trees from the wild. The color change in maples indicates a good time to collect not only deciduous trees, but their coniferous counterparts as well. Plan a nice fall excursion into the countryside. You will enjoy beautiful color, ideal mild temperatures, and the knowledge that trees you dig up will survive the ordeal. Be sure it's legal and that you have permission to dig from your chosen spot.

will weaken and die. An overactive branch can kill the branch below it. This could start a chain reaction in which the tree designs itself instead of your designing the tree.

Cut pine needles in half to promote secondary budding. In young, vigorous trees and long-needled pine species, it is advantageous to shorten pine needles by cutting them in half. This process is temporary, however, and only used for long-needled pines or rapidly growing pines in training. Bunch the pine needles up over next year's bud, and trim straight across all needles, avoiding the buds underneath. New buds will be stimulated because of the increased sunlight that touches the branch. Brown needle tips, after pruning this way, can be minimized by lightly misting the foliage regularly over the next few days.

Bring partially outdoor trees into your home. This marks the season when outdoor temperatures closely resemble indoor temperatures. It's an excellent time to bring them in. Prune away leggy growth and remove dust with a sharp blast of a hose nozzle. Prune away yellowed leaves and dead twigs. Make sure the tree is insect-free before including it with your other healthy indoor bonsai.

Prepare winter storage. It may seem too early to perform these tasks, but it's more pleasant to build cold frames in early fall rather than waiting for the weather to turn frosty. Plan ahead to make these tasks easier. Locate thermometers, extension cords, and plastic sheeting from storage. Take an inventory of what you will need. If you have several more bonsai this year than you had last year, you may need to make additional accommodations.

Watch for fall pests. I seem to get an extraordinary crop of blue jays, crows, opossums, and squirrels. Take steps to control these animals. They're preparing for winter just as you are. You may have to become a little protective and territorial when it comes to your miniature bonsai to prevent the damage that these animals can do in a relatively short time.

Slugs and snails increase their presence as fall rains arrive. Just as in spring, place a few shallow containers of beer in strategic locations around the yard.

MIDFALL

Prune fall-blooming bonsai. Many rhododendrons, azaleas, mums, and other plants are just now losing their blooms. As the flowers wilt, the plant will adjust its energy into setting seed. If these seed casings are not removed now, this energy will be misdirected. For miniature bonsai, the focus of energy should be redirected toward winter survival and next spring's growth.

Plant bonsai seeds outside. For gardens that experience winter snow, planting maple, pine, juniper, and hemlock seed couldn't be better than now. The fall rains will soak the seed coat. Winter frosts will crack the hard, protective casings, and the warm spring rain will germinate the seed. If you have natural pests, you may want to sow this seed in a protective box instead of directly in the ground.

Apply bone meal. The trace minerals in bone meal are varied and complex. It will benefit the plants' roots as well as future blossoms. Gently scrape the bonsai soil surface and water in about one handful per 30-inch plant.

Begin the fall cleanup process. Pick up fall leaves as soon as you can. Remove these to a mulch pile or haul them away. Move the bonsai around on the benches to avoid algae that may form under the pot. A final spray of fungicide will protect the fall leaves of citrus and stone-fruited trees.

Water only as needed. Bonsai that are still growing will tell you by showing dryness. Ignore the others. Do not water everything just because it's convenient.

Protect all tropicals. By now, all semi-indoor bonsai should be in their winter quarters indoors. An overnight frost can damage them severely.

Transplant and root-prune prebonsai growing in the ground. Look at your bonsai materials in the ground and examine their roots. Prune away heavy, long roots, and maintain short compact, white root hairs. Loosen the ground all around the planting area. Remove weeds, moss, and small stones. Replant the potential bonsai a bit higher than it was before. Mound soil generously around the trimmed root ball and water well.

Check branch wires again. At this time of the year, another surge in branch diameter is happening. The plant is storing sugars and starches for the winter, so it's filling its coffers with reserve energy, causing the tissues to swell quickly. This may be the best time to rewire bonsai because you can take this swelling into consideration and allow for the future expansion of spring growth as well.

Fertilize with 0–10–10. Fall color will improve, root development will be enhanced, and spring buds will be more numerous.

LATE FALL

Make the first application of lime sulfur. As the leaves on the deciduous bonsai fall, clean up the debris immediately. Maintain the ultimate in cleanliness around your benches. Water only when necessary, and use forceful jets of water to clean off foliage and residues under the pots. Pick off the last half dozen lingering leaves on your maples, and apply the first dose of lime sulfur as soon as you can. Do not allow the spray to drip into the pots; it's toxic.

Take photographs and make drawings of your trees. This will be the first opportunity to compare your trees with records made last year. Are your deciduous trees getting thicker trunks? Are they getting the beautiful twigginess so important to the illusion of age?

Make preparations for alternate storage of bonsai. What if there's a hailstorm tonight? Have you made contingency plans for your valuable trees? In case of frost, your cold frames should be ready, your benches prepared for bonsai under them, your seedling and cutting beds protected, and your sensitive species inside the house.

Do no wiring, no fertilizing, no transplanting, no collecting and no pruning. This just about sums up late fall. Divert your attention to the things you can control. Your pine will appreciate unseasonal sun. Group together those trees that require similar winter care. Construct new benches for next year. Build outdoor stands for better display.

Species Checklist

This chapter provides specific information about the five most important factors that control the life of your bonsai—soil type, the best way to prune, whether the plant is an indoor or outdoor plant, the most common pests it attracts, and the amount of sun it will tolerate. The table that follows contains most species of plants that could conceivably be used for bonsai. This is not so much a recommendation of species as much as the recognition that people often attempt to use certain cultivars or varieties within these species as bonsai material. To the right of each species, please notice that a letter appears in each column. These letters will direct you to the proper section bearing the same letter.

Species Checklist

Species	Bonsai Soil Type	Pruning Technique	Indoor Outdoor	Common Pests	Sunlight Tolerance
Abelia	A	M	Q	S,W	Y
Abies	D,E	G	R	U,V	X
Acacia	D	P	Q	S,U	Y
Acer	B	J	R	S,T,U,W	Y
Acharas	A	N	P	S	Z
Adenium	A	N	P	S	Z
Aesculus	C	M	R	S,V	X
Agonis	C	K	R	S	X
Aizoaceae	E	O	R	V	X
Albizia	C	M	R	U	X
Alnus	B	K	R	S,T	X
Andromeda	A	K	R	V	Y
Annona	B	K	Q	S,U,V	Y
Apple	C	L	R	S,T,U,V	X
Aralia	A	M	P,Q	S,U	Y
Araucaria	A	M	Q	U	Y
Arbutus	A	K	R	S,U	Y
Arctostaphylos	B	K	R	U	Y
Ardisia	A	K	P	S,U	Z
Aucuba	A	K	R	S,U	Y
Averrhoa	A	K	P	S	Z
Avocado	C	K	Q	S,U	Y
Azalea	A	K	R	V	Y

Species	Bonsai Soil Type	Pruning Technique	Indoor Outdoor	Common Pests	Sunlight Tolerance
Azara	B	K	Q	U	Y
Bamboo	B	O	Q		X
Beaucarnea	B	N	Q	S	Y
Berberis	B	K	R	U	X
Betula	B	K	R	S,T,U,V	Y
Bougainvillea	B	K	Q	U	Y
Bribotrya	B	K	P	S	Z
Bucida	B	K	P	S,U	Y
Bursera	B	K	P	S	Y
Buxus	B	K	R	S,U	Y
Cactus	E	N	Q		Y
Calliandra	B	J	P	S	Y
Calocedrus	D	H	R	U	X
Camellia	C	K	R	U,V	Y
Carissa	B	K	Q	U	Y
Carmona	B	K	Q	U	Y
Carpinus	B	K	R	S,T,U,V	Y
Cassia	B	M	Q	S,U	Y
Castanea	C	K	R	S,T,U,V	Y
Casuarina	C	F	R	U	Y
Ceanothus	C	K	R	S	Y
Cedrela	C	M	R	S,U	Y
Cedrus	D	G	R	U	X
Celtis	C	K	R	S,U	Y
Cephalotaxus	C	G	R	U	Y
Ceratonia	A	K	P	S	Y,Z
Cercidiphyllum	C	J	R	S,U	Y
Cercidium	C	K	R	U	Y
Cercis	C	K	R	S,T	Y
Cercocarpus	C	K	R	U	X
Cestrum	C	K	R	S,U	Y
Chaenomeles	C	L	R	S,U	Y

Species	Bonsai Soil Type	Pruning Technique	Indoor Outdoor	Common Pests	Sunlight Tolerance
Chamaecyparis	D	H	R	U	Y
Chamaedorea	B	M	P	U	Z
Chamaerops	D	M	R	U	Y
Chionanthus	C	K	R	S,U	Y
Chrysanthemum	B	K	R	S,U,W	Y
Cibotium	A	M	Q		Y
Cinnamomum	C	K	R	S,U	Y
Citrus	C	K	Q	S,U	Y
Cleyera	C	K	R	S,U	Y
Coffea	C	J	Q	S	Y
Comarostaphylus	C	K	Q	S	Y
Cornus	B	L	R	S,U	Y
Corokia	B	K	R	S	Y
Cotoneaster	C	L	R	S,U	Y
Crab Apple	C	L	R	S,U	Y
Crataegus	C	K	R	S,U	Y
Cryptocarya	B	J	R	U	Y
Cryptomeria	D	H	R	U	Y
Cuphea	A	K	P	U	Z
Cupressocyparis	D	H	R	U	Y
Cupressus	D	H	R	U	Y
Currant	C	J	R	S	Y
Cycas	C	M	R	U	Y
Cytisus	B	K	P,Q	U	Y,Z
Daphne	B	K	R	S,T,U	Y
Echeveria	E	O	R		Z
Elaeagnus	C	K	R	S,U	Y
Equisetum	A	O	R		Y
Erica	B	K	R		Y
Eugenia	B	K	P,Q	S	Z
Euonymus	B	K	R	S	Y
Eurya	A	K	P	S	Z

Species	Bonsai Soil Type	Pruning Technique	Indoor Outdoor	Common Pests	Sunlight Tolerance
Fagus	B	K	R	S,T,U	Y
Ficus	B	N	Q	U	Y,Z
Forsythia	B	L	R	S	Y
Fraxinus	C	M	R	S,T,U	Y
Fuchsia	B	K	Q	S	Y
Gardenia	B	J	Q	S,U	Y
Ginkgo	C	K	R		Y
Guaiacum	A	K	P,Q	S,U,V	Y,Z
Gymnocladus	B	M	R	S	Y
Hedera	B	K	R	S	Y
Hibiscus	A	K	P,Q	S	Y,Z
Ilex	C	K	R	S,U	Y
Ixora	A	K	P,Q	S	Y,Z
Juniperus	E	H	R	U	X
Kalmia	A	K	R	S,U	Y
Laburnum	B	M	R	S,T,U	Y
Lagerstroemia	C	K	R	S	Y
Larix	D	I	R	U,V	Y
Laurus	B	K	R	S,U,V	Y
Lavandula	B	J	R		Y
Leptospermum	B	K	R	S,U	Y
Leucothoe	A	K	R	S	Y
Ligustrum	B	K	R	S,U	Y
Liquidambar	C	K	R	S,T,U	Y
Lithocarpus	B	K	R	S,U	Y
Luma	C	J	R	U	Y
Macadamia	A	K	Q	U	Y,Z
Magnolia	B	K	R	S,U	Y
Malus	C	L	R	S,T,U,V	Y
Melia	C	J	R	U	Y
Metasequoia	A	I	R	U	Y
Morus	B	K	R	U	Y

Species	Bonsai Soil Type	Pruning Technique	Indoor Outdoor	Common Pests	Sunlight Tolerance
Myrica	B	K	R	S	Y
Myrsine	B	K	R	S,U	Y
Myrtus	C	K	R	S	Y
Nandina	A	O	R		Y
Nicodemia	B	K	P	U	Y,Z
Nothofagus	B	K	R		Y
Nyssa	B	K	R	S	Y
Olea	C	K	R	S	Y
Osmanthus	A	J	R	S,U	Y
Oxydendrum	A	J	R	S,U	Y
Parrotia	C	K	R	S	Y
Pelargonium	A	K	P,Q	S	Y,Z
Photinia	B	M	R	S	Y
Phylica	A	K	P	S	Z
Physocarpus	B	K	R		Y
Picea	D,E	G	R	U	X
Pieris	A	K	R	S,U	Y
Pinus	D,E	F	R	U	X
Pistachia	B	M	R	S,U	Y
Pittosporum	B	M	R	S,U	Y
Platanus	B	K	R	S,T,U,V	Y
Platycladus	D	H	R	S,U	Y
Plum	C	L	R	S,T,U,V	Y
Podocarpus	C	M	Q,R	S,U	Y,Z
Polyscias	A	J	P	S	Z
Populus	B	K	R	S,T,U,V	Y
Portulacaria	E	N	Q,R		Y,Z
Potentilla	B	K	R	S	Y
Prosopis	D	K	R	U	Y
Prune	C	L	R	S,U	Y
Prunus	C	L	R	S,U	Y
Pseudolarix	D	I	R		Y

Species	Bonsai Soil Type	Pruning Technique	Indoor Outdoor	Common Pests	Sunlight Tolerance
Pseudotsuga	D	G	R	U,V	X
Psidium	A	K	P,Q	S,U	Y,Z
Pumica	C	J	Q,R	S,U	Y
Pyracantha	C	L	R	S,T,U,V	Y
Pyrus	C	L	R	S,T,U,V	Y
Quercus	E	K	R	U	Y
Raphiolepis	A	K	P,Q	S,U	Y,Z
Rhamnus	C	J	R	S,U	Y
Rhododendron	A	L	R	S,U	Y
Ribes	B	K	R	S	Y
Rosa	C	L	R	S,T,U,V	Y
Rosmarinus	B	K	Q,R		Y,Z
Salix	B	K	R	S,T,U,V,W	Y
Salvia	B	K	R		Y
Sambulus	B	K	R	S	Y
Schefflera	A	M,N	P,Q	S,U	Y,Z
Schinus	C	M	R	U	Y
Sciadopitys	A	F	Q,R	S,U	Y
Sequoia	A	I	R	S,U	Y
Serissa	B	K	P,Q	U	Y,Z
Sophora	B	K	P,Q	U	Y,Z
Sorbus	C	M	R	U	Y
Syrax	B	K	R	S,U	Y
Syringa	A	K	R	S	Y
Syzygium	C	K	R	S	Y
Tamarix	B	M	R	S,U	Y
Taxodium	A	M	Q,R	S	Y
Taxus	C	G	R	U	Y
Thuja	D	H	R	S,U	Y
Tilia	B	K	R	S,U	Y
Trachelospermum	A	K	P	S	Y,Z
Tsuga	D	G	R	U,V	X

Species	Bonsai Soil Type	Pruning Technique	Indoor Outdoor	Common Pests	Sunlight Tolerance
Ulmus	B	K	R	S,T,U,V	Y
Vaccinium	A	K	R	S,U	Y
Viburnum	B	K	R	U	Y
Weigela	B	J	R	S	Y
Wisteria	B	L,M	Q,R	U	Y
Wrigthia	A	K	P,Q	S,V	Y,Z
Zelkova	B	K	R	S,T,U	Y
Ziziphus	C	K	R	S,T,U	Y

SOIL TYPES

Bonsai Soil Type A

This soil type is ideal for small trees and shrubs that grow under the canopy of larger climactic trees. The tall trees shed their leaves and needles each year, forming a rich blanket of compost on the forest floor. This relatively thin layer of humus supports a large variety of deciduous and evergreen shrubs and small trees. Their roots tend to be shallow, finely textured, and rather spongy in appearance.

Eighty percent of this soil should be made up of aged woody products, such as bark, sawdust, hardwood chips, leaf mold, and the like. Add about 20 percent soil vermiculite, mica, kitty litter, or other inorganic soil amendments to provide a mineral source and to increase sustained friability of the mix. Transplant or repot these species often because the high organic soil content decomposes rapidly.

Bonsai Soil Type B

This soil is made for common deciduous trees. They are similar in their needs and habitat. They're found at most altitudes wherever moisture is available on a predictable basis. They are quite seasonal and, therefore, thrive in the moderate to cold climates of our globe. Their roots stretch out considerably in their quest for both moisture and nutrients. Transplanting is required after just two years.

Mix this soil with 60 percent coarse peat, bark, rotted hardwood chips, or aged sawdust, all carefully screened to remove smaller particles. Add to this, 40 percent mineral supplement, coarse sand, decomposed rock, mica, perlite, vermiculite, hard clay, or pumice. The tree's roots will encircle the pot quickly; so, check the drain holes often.

Bonsai Soil Type C

This soil type is reserved for tough fruiting and flowering trees that grow in miserable soil in nature. These trees are not pampered, as delicate as their blooms are. We find them growing in spartan conditions in the wild—along rock ledges, in high plains country, and in impenetrable thickets. They are loved for their blossoms and their fruits, but they should not be pampered.

Their soil mix should be well screened. Only the coarsest materials should be utilized for maximum drainage. A good balanced blend of half organic and half inorganic sources is best. Coarse peat should be used sparingly in favor of wood chips and bark that won't decompose as rapidly. Similarly, leaf mold will make the soil too heavy in about a year. Mix in a generous amount, up to 50 percent, of coarse mason's sand, kitty litter, decomposed granite, pumice, lava cinders, or vermiculite. Their roots do not care to be disturbed. Make your soil coarse enough so that you do not have to transplant for three years after repotting. Annual application of bone meal is imperative.

Bonsai Soil Type D

This soil type suits most conifers, including deciduous conifers found at higher elevations. Hardy evergreen shrubs that line gorges, beaches, and windy cliffs are also favored by this mix. These trees are sun-tolerant plants that thrive in wind, rain, snow, and mild drought. They are found at all altitudes from sea level to 4,000 feet.

These plants grow primarily in rock that has decomposed over time. Seventy percent of the soil should contain sand, perlite, vermiculite, mica, pumice, volcanic ash, lava cinders, or crushed rock. These plants need a small portion of soil made up of organic debris, however. Add 30 percent leaf mold, rotten needles, old sawdust, or a combination of bark and manure, but add them sparingly and mix them well into the soil. The roots of these plants tolerate a little surface exposure and will form nice character if allowed to grow bark. Transplant these trees every four years.

Bonsai Soil Type E

This soil is best for high-altitude desert plants such as cactus, succulents, and drought-tolerant species. These plants are nature's wonders. We see them struggling against all adversity in mountains, cliffs, and arid areas. They survive because of their ability to shut down during hard times. When moisture is present and conditions are favorable, they have the ability to quickly break dormancy and take advantage of the opportunity to grow.

Ninety percent of this soil mix is decomposed rock of some kind. Try to collect this rock when you visit the desert or mountains. It may be pumice, sandstone flakes, mica, vermiculite, coarse sand, lava cinders, or volcanic debris. Add only enough needles, leaves, or mulch to make the soil complete. This soil type needs about 10 percent of these organic components.

PRUNING TECHNIQUES

Pruning Technique F

The pine family grows by sending out annual new growth called a candle. Dominant candles should be removed in their entirety in early spring as soon as it is possible without damaging adjacent candles. The remaining candles are allowed to lengthen until the individual needles just start to separate from each other. If large, gently twist off most of this candle. If medium size, pinch off only half. If small, allow it to grow.

Pruning Technique G

This family of plants includes the spruce, fir, and hemlock. New growth in early spring is protected by a sheath. When this thin covering naturally falls off, you'll see an oblong-shaped concentration of bright new needles trying to unfold. Remove all these buds in their entirety; they're young and tender. Grasp them between thumb and forefinger and gently pull forward, and they'll separate without much force. This early-spring pinching will start a series of efforts by the tree to grow. New growth will appear everywhere. Pick and choose the buds that you desire and eliminate the buds that you do not want.

Pruning Technique H

This technique is appropriate for most needle junipers, cypress, cedar, and arborvitae. New growth appears in midspring, and it's characterized by the gradual appearance of a light chartreuse growth on the outer extensions of the branches or apex. Allow this growth to continue until it is about 1 inch long; then completely remove it to stimulate lots of new buds within the branch. This pruning technique requires you to prune constantly during the growing season, even up to early fall.

Pruning Technique I

Prune these deciduous conifers only after the branch has grown about 2 inches long. Early-spring growth is too succulent to shape or wire. Rub out unwanted buds as soon as they appear. Allow branch growth to extend several inches before pinching back the tip; the branch will then divide. Secondary growth should be allowed to extend for 2 inches before pruning again; then, this branch will divide once again. Give these plants as much sun as they can stand without sunburn. High sunlight will help compact the new growth.

Pruning Technique J

This is the pruning appropriate for any deciduous tree that grows leaves opposite one another along the branch. The new growth in spring will produce a regular predictable pattern of leaves. Two leaves will first appear as a curled-up clump of foliage, which then opens up. The next two leaves will appear shortly after, but rotated 90 degrees along the branch with respect to the first two leaves. Select the pair of leaves growing horizontally to each other instead of vertically to each other. Prune just in front of them when the branch extends itself farther. Before cutting, make sure that new growth has extended itself at least two pairs of leaves beyond where you want to cut, enhancing back budding. If you prune after only one pair of leaves has emerged beyond the pruning site, new growth will only occur at the branch tip. If you wait until the third or fourth pair of leaves appears, the internodes will be too long.

Pruning Technique K

These deciduous trees have alternate leaves along the branch. The leaf direction indicates the future direction of the new bud. If you do not want growth upward, for example, do not prune just beyond an upward-facing leaf stem. If you desire growth to extend toward the right, prune just beyond a leaf that faces in that direction. You will find that leaves will sprout in a very regular fashion such as up, down, right, left, up, down, right, left. You'll have plenty of opportunities to sculpt your tree properly.

Pruning Technique L

This is a very specialized pruning technique that's appropriate to any of the rose family and includes the blackberry, wild rose, cotoneaster, pyracantha, apple, and dogwood, among others. The pruning of this group requires that you study differences between vegetative and fruiting growth. Fruiting growth, unfortunately, always appears on aging vegetative growth; so, you can appreciate the problem. You must maintain some select vegetative growth or no fruit will appear. I recommend pruning half the branches on the tree heavily each year. Then the following year, prune back the other half. You can tell by the shape of the new growth which branches were pruned last year, allowing you to avoid pruning away blooms and blooms in progress.

Pruning Technique M

These trees produce what look like a number of leaves on a branch, but watch out. They're actually producing only one leaf. Their "leaves" are really a cluster of what *look* like individual leaves but are not. Do not make the mistake of thinking you can control growth by pinching or pruning between these so-called leaves, because nothing will happen. Wait until this tree produces an-

other series of leaves beyond the first series, when you have two actual leaves. Then you may prune off one of these to get the branch to divide.

Pruning Technique N

This method is used on tropical trees with a milky, latex sap. Growth is constant since these trees are typically grown in rather sheltered locations, like a greenhouse or atrium. Do not use a sharp pruning tool since you will only make the plant "bleed" to excess. Rather, use a dull knife, poultry scissors, or wire cutters. On large specimens, I prefer to prune with needle-nosed pliers because the pruning injury is great, therefore, creating a massive load of traumatic acid in the plant. Healing is stimulated by the trauma and the sap is stopped. An extremely sharp knife will cause the maple to produce gallons of maple syrup. The blow from a dull ax will readily heal over. The same principle is at work here with these tropicals. Did you ever notice how long it takes to heal a cut from a razor blade?

Pruning Technique O

These bonsai are members of the grass, lily, or tuber families. They are propagated by division, and pruning consists of removing distracting growth to improve style. When old growth becomes yellow and unproductive, remove it below ground level with root trimmers.

INDOOR OR OUTDOOR ENVIRONMENTS

Indoor or Outdoor P

These plants grow near the equator. They do not want to feel the seasons. They want a constant source of bright, indirect light and a modest fluctuation in temperature from 80° F during the day to 50° F at night. They grow constantly and must be pruned constantly. Their leaves require copious quantities of water, nutrients, and oxygen. They abhor movement and a new location will send them into temporary shock. Do not touch them because your hands have oils that will damage the leaves.

Indoor or Outdoor Q

These plants from near the equator feel the seasons but do not tolerate frost. In colder climates, these plants may become temporary house guests during the winter months. They tolerate strong sunlight through a window because they've spent the summer outdoors. In late spring, move them outdoors again, trim off the gangly growth that occurred during their indoor stay, and gradually acclimate them to the sun again.

Indoor or Outdoor R

These plants are native to the colder, seasonal parts of the world. They constitute the largest group of bonsai, around 90 percent. This group includes most conifers and all deciduous trees. You need to protect them from extreme heat and extreme cold only because they're in containers.

COMMON PESTS

Common Pests S

These plants are highly susceptible to aphids, white fly, thrips, mites, mealybugs, and other soft-bodied insects. The plants' succulent new growth is an easy prey for these insects which are looking for a convenient source of sweet sap.

Common Pests T

These plants are water-loving deciduous trees. The caterpillar is always a threat, starting in late spring and extending to midsummer.

Common Pests U

These plants are prone to attack by a group of insects known by their protective coatings or armor. This group of pests includes the spittle bugs, scale insects, and woolly aphids, among others.

Common Pests V

These plants will likely experience an attack of boring insects. This group of insects, of course, includes tiny pests that burrow into dead wood. Insects that hide at night inside the tree are also included in this category since the treatment is the same. (See chapter 8.)

Common Pests W

Protect these plants from slugs and snails. Their foliage is very tasty to these creatures; so, measures must be taken to prevent extensive damage to the plants.

SUNLIGHT TOLERANCES

Sunlight Tolerance X

This group of plants will enjoy sun all day long. Unusual circumstances may require shade, for example, during vacation time or unusually hot weather. For the most part, however, let them bask in the sun's rays year-round. Rotate the plants to even out the strength of the new growth. Avoid watering the foliage except for an occasional cleansing blast from the garden hose.

Sunlight Tolerance Y

This group of plants does not like the full heat of the sun after 1 P.M. in the summer. The leaves will curl, turn brittle, and scald if exposed to this kind of sun. Once the thermometer rises above 85° F, these plants prefer the mottled sun-shade under the spreading canopy of a large shade tree. Give these plants plenty of water in the hottest months. Rinse off the foliage weekly.

Sunlight Tolerance Z

This group of plants would prefer never getting direct rays from the sun. They are native to areas where they grow deep in the forest with plenty of moisture and humidity. Bright, indirect light from the sun is ideal. Temperatures are preferred between 65° F and 80° F. Sometimes, the addition of artificial grow lights is necessary for success. Do not place these plants in the sun for any reason, not even for a few minutes; they will sunburn quickly.

Japanese Maple, *Acer palmatum* 'Shishigashira'

Plants Recommended for Miniature Bonsai

Abies amabilis	Pacific Silver Fir, Cascade Fir	*Acer palmatum*	Japanese Maple
Abies balsamea 'Nana'	Dwarf Balsam Fir	*Acer palmatum* 'Arakawa'	Arakawa Maple
Abies koreana	Korean Fir	*Acer palmatum* 'Atropurpureum'	Atropurpureum Maple
Abies lasiocarpa	Alpine Fir		
Abies lasiocarpa 'Arizonica'	Cork Fir	*Acer palmatum* 'Beni Hime'	*Beni Hime* Japanese Maple
Acacia baileyana	Golden Mimosa, Cootamundra	*Acer palmatum* 'Bloodgood'	Japanese Bloodgood Maple
		Acer palmatum 'Butterfly'	Japanese Butterfly Maple
Acer aureum 'Shirasawassum'	Shirasawassum Japanese Maple	*Acer palmatum* 'Ever Red'	Red Japanese Maple
		Acer palmatum 'Kiyo Hime'	*Kiyo Hime* Maple
Acer buergerianum	Trident Maple	*Acer palmatum* 'Koshimino'	Dwarf Japanese Maple
Acer campestre	Hedge Maple, Field Maple	*Acer palmatum* 'Linearilobum'	Thread-leaf Japanese Maple
Acer campestre 'Compacta'	Compact Hedge Maple		
Acer capillipes	Japanese Red Maple	*Acer palmatum* 'Masukagami'	Masukagami Japanese Maple
Acer circinatum	Vine Maple		
Acer ginnala	Amur Maple	*Acer palmatum* 'Omato'	Omato Japanese Maple
Acer griseum	Paperbark Maple	*Acer palmatum* 'Orangeola'	Orangeola Japanese Maple
Acer japonicum	Full-Moon Maple, Japanese Maple	*Acer palmatum* 'Ruby Lace'	Ruby-Lace Japanese Maple
		Acer palmatum 'Sangokaku'	Coral-Barked Maple
Acer japonicum 'Aconitifolium'	Laceleaf Full-Moon Maple	*Acer palmatum* 'Sanguineum'	Sanguineum Japanese Maple
		Acer palmatum 'Seki Mori'	*Seki Mori* Japanese Maple
Acer japonicum 'Aureum'	Golden Full-Moon Maple	*Acer palmatum* 'Shigitasu-sawa'	*Shigatisu-sawa* Japanese Maple
Acer oblongum	Evergreen Maple		

Japanese Maple, *Acer palmatum* 'Suminagashi'

Japanese Maple, *Acer palmatum* 'Seki Mori'

Japanese Maple, *Acer palmatum* 'Waterfall'

Acer palmatum 'Shigure Bato'	*Shigure Bato* Japanese Maple	*Acer truncatum*	Chinese Maple
Acer palmatum 'Shishigashira'	Dwarf Crinkled-Leaved Maple	*Albizia julibrissin*	Mimosa, Silk Tree
		Alnus tenuifolia	Mountain Alder
Acer palmatum 'Suminagashi'	Suminagashi Japanese Maple	*Araucaria heterophylla* (*A. excelsa*)	Araucaria Pine, Norfolk Island Pine
Acer palmatum 'Villa Taranto'	Villa Taranto Japanese Maple	*Arctostaphylos manzanita*	Manzanita, Bearberry
Acer palmatum 'Viride'	Viride Japanese Maple	*Ardisia crenata*	Spear Flower, Coralberry, Spiceberry
Acer palmatum 'Waterfall'	Waterfall Japanese Maple		
Acer paxii	Lobed Evergreen Maple	*Arundinaria disticha*	Dwarf Fern-Leaf Bamboo
Acer rubrum	Red Maple	*Arundinaria marmorea*	Dwarf Black Bamboo
Acer saccharum grandidentatum	Rocky Mountain Maple	*Bambusa glaucescens* (*B. multiplex*)	Hedge Bamboo
		Berberis aurea	Barberry
Acer tataricum	Tatarian Maple	*Betula nana*	Dwarf Arctic Birch
Acer triflorum	Japanese Maple	*Betula pendula* 'Fastigiata'	Pyramidal White Birch

Betula pendula 'Lanciniata'	Cutleaf Weeping Birch
Betula pendula 'Purpurea'	Purple Birch
Betula pendula 'Trost's Dwarf'	Trost's Dwarf Birch
Betula platyphylla 'Japonica'	Japanese White Birch
Bougainvillea glabra	Lesser Bougainvillea
Bucida spinosa	Dwarf Spiny Black Olive
Bursera simaruba	West India Birch, Gumbo-Limbo, Gum Elemi
Buxus microphylla 'Compacta'	Dwarf Boxwood
Buxus microphylla 'Koreana'	Korean Boxwood
Buxus microphylla 'Morris Midget'	Morris Midget Boxwood
Calliandra	Powderpuff
Calocedrus decurrens	California Incense Cedar
Camellia sasanqua	Sasanqua Camellia
Camellia sinensis	Tea, Tea Plant
Camellia vernalis	Vernalis Camellia
Carissa macrocarpa	Christ's Thorn, Natal Plum
Carpinus betulus	European Hornbeam, European Ironwood
Carpinus caroliniana	American Hornbeam, Blue Beech, Water Beech

Japanese Maple, *Acer palmatum* 'Shigitasu-sawa'

Japanese Maple, *Acer japonicum*

Japanese Maple, *Acer palmatum* 'Shigure Bato'

Contorted Larch, *Larix decidua* 'Diane'

Japanese Maple, *Acer palmatum* 'Ruby Lace'

Carpinus turczaninovii	Turkish Hornbeam
Cassia marilandica	Cassia, Wild Senna
Cedrus brevifolia	Cyprus Cedar
Cedrus libani	Cedar-of-Lebanon
Cedrus libani 'Nana'	Dwarf Cedar-of-Lebanon
Celtis sinensis	Japanese Hackberry
Cercis chinensis	Chinese Redbud
Cercocarpus ledifolius	Curl-Leaf Mountain Mahogany
Chaenomeles japonica	Japanese Flowering Quince
Chamaecyparis lawsoniana 'Ellwoodii Improved'	Ellwood Cypress
Chamaecyparis lawsoniana 'Minima Glauca'	Dwarf Blue Cypress
Chamaecyparis nootkatensis 'Compacta'	Dwarf Alaska Yellow Cedar, Dwarf Nootka Cypress
Chamaecyparis obtusa 'Filicoides'	Fernspray Cypress
Chamaecyparis obtusa 'Kosteri'	Koster Cypress
Chamaecyparis obtusa 'Nana'	Dwarf Hinoki Cypress, Dwarf Japanese False Cypress
Chamaecyparis pisifera	Sawara False Cypress
Chamaecyparis pisifera 'Filifera'	Threadbranch Cypress
Chamaecyparis thyoides 'Andelyensis Conica'	Andelyensis Conica Cypress, Andelyensis White Cedar
Chrysanthemum frutescens	Marguerite, White Marguerite, Paris Daisy
Chrysanthemum morifolium	Florist's Chrysanthemum, Mum
Cinnamomum camphora	Camphor Tree
Citrus microcarpa	Citrus Tree
Clematis montana	Anemone Clematis
Coffea arabica and *robusta*	Coffee Bush

White Pine, *Pinus strobus* 'Globosa'

Canadian Hemlock, *Tsuga canadensis* 'Pendula'

Japanese Maple, *Acer palmatum* 'Orangeola'

Cornus kousa	Korean Dogwood
Cornus mas	Cornelian Cherry, Sorbet
Corokia cotoneaster	Corokia
Corylus avellana 'Contorta'	Harry Lauder's Walking Stick
Corylus maxima 'Purpurea'	Purple Filbert, Purple Hazelnut
Cotoneaster congestus	Congested Cotoneaster
Cotoneaster microphyllus 'Cochleatus'	Dwarf Creeping Cotoneaster
Cotoneaster microphyllus 'Thymifolius'	Thyme-Leaf Cotoneaster
Crassula argentea 'Crosby's Dwarf'	Dwarf Jade, Jade Tree, Dollar Plant, Cauliflower Ears, Chinese Rubber Plant

Crassula tetragona	Succulent Pine, Miniature Pine Tree, Chinese Pine
Crataegus ambigua	Russian Hawthorn, Russian Thorn Apple
Cryptomeria japonica 'Bandai-sugi'	Conical Cryptomeria
Cryptomeria japonica 'Jundai-sugi'	Globular Cryptomeria
Cryptomeria japonica 'Pygmaea'	Dwarf Cryptomeria
Cryptomeria japonica 'Tansu'	Japanese Cedar, Tansu Cryptomeria
Cuphea hyssopifolia	False Heather, Japanese Myrtle, Elfin Herb
Cupressus forbesii	Tecate Cypress
Cupressus macrocarpa	Monterey Cypress
Cytisus racemosus	Cystisus, Broom
Dionaea muscipula	Venus Flytrap
Eugenia brasiliensis	Brazil Cherry
Eurya emarginata 'Microphylla'	Japanese Fern Tree

White Spruce, *Picea abies* 'Verigata'

Eurya japonica	Japanese Elderberry
Fagus sylvatica 'Asplenifolia'	Cut-Leaf Beech
Fagus sylvatica 'Atropurpurea' ('Atropunicea')	Copper Beech
Fagus sylvatica 'Lanciniata'	Laceleaf Beech, Fern-Leaf Beech, Cut-Leaf Beech
Fagus sylvatica 'Rohanii'	Oak-Leaf Beech
Fagus sylvatica 'Spathiana'	Purple Beech
Fagus sylvatica 'Tricolor'	Tricolor Beech
Fagus sylvatica 'Zlatia'	Golden Beech
Ficus	Fig Tree
Fuchsia 'Isis'	Fuchsia
Fuchsia magellanica 'Macrostema'	Gracilis Fuchsia, Hardy Fuchsia
Ginkgo biloba	Maidenhair Tree
Grevillea rosmarinifolia	Rosemary Tree
Guaiacum officinale	Lignum-vitae, Pockwood Tree
Hakonechloa macra 'Aureola'	Japanese Forest Grass
Hamamelis mollis	Chinese Witch Hazel
Hedera helix	English Ivy
Hibiscus rosa-sinensis	Blacking Plant, Chinese Hibiscus, China Rose, Hawaiian Hibiscus

Dwarf Hinoki Cypress, *Chamaecyparis obtusa* 'Nana'

Japanese Maple, *Acer palmatum* 'Villa Taranto'

Blue Spruce, *Picea pungens* 'River Road'

Canadian Hemlock, *Tsuga canadensis* 'Curly'

Canadian Hemlock, *Tsuga canadensis*

Ilex crenata 'Mariesii'	Dwarf Japanese Holly, Dwarf Box-Leaved Holly
Ilex dimorphophylla	Okinawan Holly
Imperata cylindrica 'Rubra'	Japanese Blood Grass
Ixora javanica	Jungle Geranium
Juniperus chinensis 'Blaauw'	Blue Shimpaku, Blue Juniper
Juniperus chinensis 'Parsonii'	Prostrate Juniper
Juniperus chinensis 'Procumbens Nana'	Japanese Green Mound Juniper
Juniperus chinensis 'Sargentii'	Shimpaku
Juniperus chinensis 'Skyrocket'	Skyrocket Juniper
Juniperus chinensis 'Torulosa'	Hollywood Juniper
Juniperus communis 'Compressa'	Dwarf Columnar Juniper
Larix decidua	European Larch
Larix decidua 'Diane'	Contorted Larch
Larix kaempferi	Japanese Larch
Leptospermum scoparium	Tea Tree, New Zealand Tea Tree, Manuka, Australian Myrtle

Japanese Maple, *Acer palmatum* 'Masukagami'

Japanese Maple, *Acer palmatum* 'Viride'

Ligustrum japonicum	Japanese Privet, Wax-Leaf Privet	*Narcissus* 'Minimus' (*N. asturiensis*)	Dwarf Daffodil
Lonicera nitida	Chinese Honeysuckle	*Narcissus* 'Triandrus'	Angel's Tears Daffodil
Magnolia parviflora (*M. sieboldii*)	Oyama Magnolia	*Nicodemia diversifolia* (*Buddleia diversifolia*)	Butterfly Bush
Malus 'Dorothea'	Yellow Crab Apple (pink flowers)	*Nothofagus antarctica*	Antarctic Beech
Malus floribunda	Japanese Flowering Crab Apple, Purple Chokeberry, Showy Crab Apple	*Nothofagus cunninghamii*	Pelargonium, Geranium Beech
Malus 'Radiant'	Red Crab Apple (red flowers)	*Olea europaea* 'Little Ollie'	Dwarf Olive
		Parrotica persica	Persian Beech
Malus zumi 'Calocarpa'	Red Crab Apple (white flowers)	*Phoenix roebelenii*	Pygmy Date Palm, Miniature Date Palm
Myrtus communis 'Microphylla'	Dwarf Myrtle, German Myrtle, Polish Myrtle	*Phylica ericoides*	Phylica
		Picea abies 'Mucronata'	Dwarf Spruce
		Picea abies 'Pygmaea'	Pygmy Norway Spruce

Japanese Maple, *Acer palmatum* 'Bloodgood'

Japanese Maple, *Acer palmatum* 'Sangokaku'

Weeping White Pine, *Pinus strobus* 'Pendula'

Seiju Elm, *Ulmus parvifolia* 'Seiju'

Picea abies 'Verigata'	White Spruce
Picea englemannii	Dwarf Alberta Spruce
Picea pungens 'River Road'	Blue Spruce
Pieris japonica 'Compacta'	Dwarf Andromeda, Dwarf Lily-of-the-Valley Bush
Pinus albicaulis	White-Bark Pine
Pinus aristata	Bristle-Cone Pine
Pinus balfouriana	Foxtail Pine
Pinus bungeana	Lace-Bark Pine
Pinus cembroides 'Monophylla'	Blue Piñon Pine, Mexican Stone Pine
Pinus chinensis	Chinese Pistachio
Pinus contorta 'Murrayana'	Mountain Lodgepole Pine
Pinus densiflora	Japanese Red Pine
Pinus densiflora 'Umbraculifera'	Tanyosho Pine, Japanese Umbrella Pine
Pinus edulis	Piñon Pine, Nut Pine, Two-Leaved Nut Pine
Pinus flexilis	Limber Pine
Pinus halepensis	Aleppo Pine, Jerusalem Pine

Japanese Maple, *Acer palmatum* 'Ever Red'

Pinus monophylla	One-Needle Pine, Single-Leaf Piñon Pine, Stone Pine	*Potentilla fruticosa*	Shrubby Cinquefoil, Golden Hardhack, Widdy
Pinus monticola	Western White Pine	*Prunus cistena*	Dwarf Flowering Cherry, Purple-Leaf Sand Cherry
Pinus mugo mugo	Dwarf Mugo Pine	*Prunus hally jollivette*	Pink Flowering Cherry
Pinus pinea	Italian Stone Pine	*Prunus serrula*	Birch Bark Cherry
Pinus strobus	Eastern White Pine	*Prunus serrulata*	Japanese Flowering Cherry
Pinus strobus 'Globosa'	Globosa White Pine	*Prunus mume*	Japanese Flowering Apricot
Pinus strobus 'Nana'	Dwarf White Pine	*Prunus tomentosa*	Nanking Cherry, Red Fruit, Chinese Bush Fruit
Pinus strobus 'Pendula'	Weeping White Pine		
Pinus sylvestris 'Nana'	Dwarf Scotch Pine	*Prunus virginiana*	Chokecherry
Pinus thunbergiana	Japanese Black Pine	*Pseudolarix kaempferi*	Golden Larch
Pistacia	Pistachio, Mastic Tree	*Psidiuum cattleianum*	Strawberry Guava
Pittosporum tobira	Japanese Pittosporum, Australian Laurel, Mock Orange	*Punica granatum* 'Nana'	Dwarf Pomegranate
		Pyracantha	Fire Thorn
Platanus occidentalis	Buttonwood, Eastern Sycamore, American Plane Tree	*Pyracantha* 'Red Elf'	Compact Fire Thorn
		Pyrus kawakamii	Evergreen Pear
		Pyrus salicifolia 'Pendula'	Willow-Leaved Pear
Podocarpus nivalis	Alpine Yew	*Quercus dumosa*	California Scrub Oak
Populis tremuloides	Quaking Aspen, Trembling Aspen, Quiverleaf	*Quercus ilex*	Holly Oak

Japanese Maple, *Acer palmatum* 'Sanguineum'

Quercus myrsinifolia	Japanese Evergreen Oak
Quercus phellos	Willow Oak
Quercus suber	Cork Oak
Quercus vaccinifolia	Huckleberry Oak
Raphiolepis indica	Indian Hawthorn
Rhododendron 'Blue Diamond'	Lavender Rhododendron
Rhododendron 'Bow Bells'	Pink Rhododendron
Rhododendron 'Ginny Gee'	Pink to White Rhododendron
Rhododendron 'Hotel'	Yellow Rhododendron
Rhododendron kiusianum	Japanese Rhododendron
Rhododendron kurume	Azaleas (many colors)
Rhododendron mucronulatum	Deciduous Purple Rhododendron
Rhododendron 'Nancy Evans'	Orange Rhododendron
Rhododendron satsuki	Azaleas (many colors)
Rhododendron 'Trilby'	Red Rhododendron
Rhodohypoxis baurii	Rhodohypoxis (Dwarf Bulbs)
Rosmarinus officinalis	Wild Rosemary
Salix purpurea 'Nana'	Dwarf Alaskan Blue Willow, Dwarf Purple Osier, Dwarf Basket Willow
Salix sachalinensis 'Setsuka'	Setsuka Willow
Schefflera arboricola	Hawaiian Elf Schefflera, Umbrella Tree
Serissa foetida	Chinese Snow Rose
Sorbus reducta	Dwarf Mountain Ash
Sorbus tianshanica	Turkestan Mountain Ash
Styrax japonicus	Japanese Snowbell
Syringa koreana	Korean Lilac
Taxodium distichum	Bald Cypress

Japanese Maple, *Acer palmatum* 'Shishigashira' summer color

Japanese Maple, *Acer palmatum* 'Beni-hime'

Taxodium mucronatum	Montezuma Cypress	*Ulmus parvifolia*	Chinese Elm
Taxus cuspidata 'Nana'	Dwarf Japanese Yew	*Ulmus parvifolia* 'Hokkaido'	Hokkaido Elm
Taxus media 'Brownii'	Brown's Yew	*Ulmus parvifolia* 'Seiju'	Seiju Elm
Thuja occidentalis 'Little Giant'	Little Giant Arborvitae	*Wisteria floribunda*	Japanese Wisteria
Thuja occidentalis 'Nana'	Dwarf Arborvitae	*Wisteria sinensis*	Chinese Wisteria
Tillia cordata	Small-Leaved European Linden	*Wrigthia (Holarrhena antidysenterica)*	Wrigthia
Trachelospermum jasminoides	Star Jasmine, Confederate Jasmine	*Zelkova serrata*	Sawleaf Zelkova, Japanese Zelkova
Tsuga canadensis	Canadian Hemlock	*Ziziphus jujuba*	Chinese Date, Common Jujube, Chinese Jujube
Tsuga canadensis 'Curly'	Curly Canadian Hemlock		
Tsuga candensis 'Pendula'	Weeping Canadian Hemlock		

Bonsai Glossary

accompaniment planting usually secondary miniature plantings, such as bulbs, grasses, or smaller species, that accompany larger, more significant bonsai and contribute to the unity of the design

acerifolius leaf form resembling a maple

adpressus pressing against; hugging plant form

air-layering the process in which roots are developed on a stem or branch above the ground

albus white color

altus tall plant form

angustifolius narrow leaf form

arboreus tree-like plant form

argenteus silvery color

armatus armed

aureus golden color

australis of Australia

azureus azure, sky blue color

baccatus berried or berry-like

ball shape *tama-zukuri*, in the shape of a ball

bankan coiled style, a spiraled trunk

barbatus barbed or bearded

bilobate divided into two lobes, as of a leaf

bipinnate doubly pinnate, as of a leaf consisting of a central axis and lateral axes to which leaflets are attached

bolt the growth of a plant too quickly to flowering at the expense of good overall development

bonkei a landscape created with sand, gravel, boats, huts, figurines, and lanterns in a large, flat tray-shaped pot with no living plants

bonseki a landscape created with mini figurines, nonliving foliage, and the appearance of water created with a mirror

borealis of the north

bract leaf-like appendage at the base of a flower, sometimes brightly colored as in poinsettia

broadleaf foliage which is neither a needle shape nor scale-like

broom style *hoki-dachi*, *hoki-zukuri*, *hokidachi*; resembling the shape of a broom, best suited to twiggy deciduous trees

bulb style *shitakusa*; perennials

bunjin, bunjinji literati style; free-form and unexplainable, disregards rules of style, design, and growth

buxifolius leaves like boxwood

caesius blue gray color

cambium a thin, formative layer consisting of xylem and phloem in all woody plants that gives rise to new cells; responsible for secondary growth and transmission of nutrients

campanulatus bell- or cup-shaped

campestris of Canada

canariensis of the Canary Islands

candidus pure white color; shiny

candle-flame shape *rosoku-zukuri*; in the shape of a candle flame, such as *arborvitae*

canus ashy gray color

capensis of the Cape of Good Hope

capitatus head-like

carneus flesh-colored, pinkish beige

catkin string of single-sex flowers, without petals, often pendulous; found on trees such as alder, birch, and willow

cereus waxy

chilensis of Chile

chinensis of China

chiu **bonsai** medium- size two-handed bonsai from 16 to 36 inches

chlorosis diseased condition in plants characterized by yellowing, frequently caused by a lack of iron

chokkan formal upright style; straight, vertical trunk

chumono **bonsai** medium-size two-handed bonsai from 10 to 18 inches

ciliaris yellow color

clustered style *tsukami-yose*; clustered group with multiple trunks springing from one tree

coccineus scarlet color

coeruleus dark blue color

coiled style *bankan*; a spiraled trunk

compactus compact, dense plant shape

compound leaf a leaf consisting of two or more leaflets

concolor one color

cone fruit of a conifer consisting of wood scales enclosing naked multiple ovules or seeds

confertus crowded, pressed-together plant shape

conifer cone-bearing plant; may be deciduous

cordatus cordate; heart-shaped

cornatus horned

crassus thick, fleshy

cruentus bloody color

culm the hollow-jointed stems of grasses, especially bamboo

cultivar cultivated variety; see *species* and *variety*

cultural dwarf manipulation of growth characteristics which results in dwarfing

cutting any plant fragment cut off for the purpose of rooting a new plant

dai-**bonsai** large four-handed bonsai from 30 to 48 inches

damping off fungus disease usually attacking cuttings or seedlings

deciduous referring to plants that drop their leaves or needles at the end of the growing season

decumbens Lying-down plant shape

decurrens running down the stem

defoliate the early removal of leaves; a common artificial technique in bonsai training

-dendron tree

dentate sharply toothed leaf margins

depressus pressed-down plant shape

desiccate to dry up or cause to dry up

dieback a progressive plant condition characterized by stem failure, starting from the tips of leaves and branches; due to disease, insect, or environment damage

discolor two colors; separate colors

dissected usually a highly intricate natural cutting of a leaf, as in *Acer palmatum dissectum*, also called laceleaf

diversi varying

double-trunk style *sokan*; two trunks attached to each other in the bottom quarter of the tree with the larger trunk displayed slightly forward of the smaller

driftwood style *sarimiki*, *sharimiki*; large areas of dead wood with desert, beach, or high-altitude appearance

drip line a circle directly under a tree that corresponds to where water drips on the ground, usually just inside the tips of the lower branches

earth-layering creating roots on a stem or branch by burying a section in the ground

edulis edible

elegans elegant, slender, willowy plant shape

elongated style *goza-kake*; exaggerated first branch balanced by a special wide pot; sometimes found over water

epiphyte a plant that grows on another for support; not to be confused with parasite

exposed-root style *ne-agari*; air space under roots that suggests erosion

eye an undeveloped growth bud

fallen-cone style *yama-yori*; hundred-tree style; hundreds of sprouts from one vicinity

fastigiatus branches erect and close together

-fer, -iferus bearing or having

five-tree style *gohon-yose*; a group planting of five trees

floridus free-flowering

formal regular, rigid, and geometric, as in formal upright design

formal cascade style *kengai*; first branch extends below the bottom edge of the pot and pot sits on a stand

formal upright style *chokkan*; straight, vertical trunk

fruticosa shrubby

fukunigashi windswept style; tree slant indicates wind direction, as though the tree were growing on a mountain or near a beach; slant may be extreme or gentle

fulgens shiny

genetic dwarf small size and other characteristics are genetically determined

genus a classification of related plants; the first word in a botanical name

glaucus covered with gray bloom

gohon-yose five-tree style; a group planting of five trees

goza-kake elongated style; exaggerated first branch balanced by a special wide pot; sometimes found over water

gracilis slender, thin, small plant shape

grandis large, showy plant shape

grass plantings *kusamomo*, including bamboo

group-planting style *yose-uye, yose-ue*; more than nine trees or any larger prime number; a grove or group planting rather than a forest

hachi-uye bonsai large six-handed bonsai from 48 to 60 inches

han-kengai semicascade style; foliage of first branch must extend below the top edge of the pot. *Kai-kengai*: vertical cascade; *gaito-kengai*: mountaintop cascade; *ito-kengai*: string cascade; *tokan-kengai*: two-trunk cascade

harden off the progressive adaptation of a tender plant to the full brunt of harsh outdoor conditions

hardy a plant that can resist cold; usually expressed as hardy to −15° F (−26° C), for example

heavy soil a term commonly used to describe clay or compacted soils

herbaceous nonwoody

hokidachi, hoki-dachi, or hoki-zukuri style resembling the shape of a broom, best suited to twiggy, deciduous trees

hollow-trunk style *sabakan*; as the heartwood rots away in some species, such as live oak or coast redwood, a hollowed-out trunk is formed

honeydew any secretion caused by sucking insects on a plant, usually attracting ants

hortensis of gardens

humilis low, small, humble plant form

humus the late stages of rotting organic material

hundred-tree style *yama-yori*, fallen-cone style; hundreds of sprouts from one vicinity

hybrid plant created by crossing two species of the same genus or two varieties of the same species

ikadabuki raft style; single tree on its side with branches trained upright as though individual trees; visually creates a forest

ilicifolius holly-like leaves

imperial bonsai large eight-handed bonsai from 60 to 80 inches

impressus impressed upon

incanus gray color

informal upright style *moyogi, tachiki*; curving upright trunk; apex is over rootage

insularis of the island

internode a section of a stem between two successive nodes

ishizuke, ishitsuke, or ishitzuke rocky-garden style characterized by entire tree planted on a rock, but no soil in the pot; possibly water, sand, or bare glaze in the bottom of the pot

jin the dead apex of a tree, usually found only on a rock, with no soil in the pot; literally means "god," symbolic of the gods' influence on nature

kabudachi sprout style, *miyama-kirishima*; characterized by sprouts developed on an old stump, a section of fallen tree, or part of a rotten log; sprouts arranged like flowers to contrast new life with old tree

kasa-zukuri umbrella shape

katade-mochi bonsai medium-size one-handed bonsai from 10 to 18 inches

kengai formal cascade style; first branch extends below the bottom edge of the pot; pot sits on a stand

keshitsubu bonsai poppy-seed-size bonsai from 1 to 3 inches

knobby-trunk style *kobukan*; healed-over sprouts, often caused by stress in nature

komono bonsai miniature one-handed bonsai from 6 to 10 inches

kusamomo grass plantings, including bamboo

kyuhon-yose nine-trunk style; a group planting of nine trees

laciniatus   fringed or with torn edges

laevigatus   smooth

lanceolate   lance-shaped

lateral   positioned at the side; an extension of a branch or a shoot

lath   usually refers to a series of wooden boards erected above plants to provide artificial shade

laurifolius   laurel-like leaves

leaching   the removal of substances from the soil by excess watering

leader   the dominant upward single central growth of a plant

leaf mold   partially decomposed leaves; not yet humus

leaf scar   the slight indentation left on a twig that remains after a leaf stalk is removed

leaflet   divisions of a leaf, either palmate (fan-shaped) or pinnate (feather-shaped)

legume   pod or seed vessel of the pea family, splitting lengthwise to release seeds

light soil   commonly referred to as sandy soil; more precisely, well-aerated soil

linear   long and narrow, with parallel sides

literati style   see *bunjin, bunjinji*

littoralis   of the seashore

lobatus   lobed; projection or division of a leaf or petal

luteus   reddish yellow color

maculatus   spotted

mame **bonsai**   miniature one-handed bonsai from 5 to 8 inches

matsu-zukuri   pine-tree shape; may also be used for deciduous trees

meristem   a formative plant tissue usually made up of small cells capable of dividing indefinitely to form similar cells or cells that differentiate to produce the definitive tissues and organs

miyama-kirishima   sprout style, *kabudachi*; characterized by sprouts developed on an old stump, a section of fallen tree, or part of a rotten log; sprouts arranged like flowers to contrast new life with old tree

mollis   soft and hairy

montanus   of the mountains

moyogi   *tachiki*, informal upright style; curving upright trunk; apex is over rootage

mucronatus   pointed

mulch   a loose organic covering over soil or used to describe the process of applying such a layer

mycorrhiza   symbiotic association of mycelium of a fungus with roots of a seed plant

nanahon-yose   seven-trunk style; a group planting of seven trees

nanus   dwarf

natural dwarf   a plant dwarfed by the forces of nature

natural style   *yomayori, yomayose*; natural, informal grouping

ne-agari   exposed-root style; air space under roots that suggests erosion

nejikan   twisted style; trunk spirals upward with growth

netsunari   root-connected style; trees sprout from long surface roots of more than one root stock; occurs naturally in willow, quince, Chinese raintree, vine maple, wild cherry

nine-trunk style   *kyuhon-yose*; a group planting of nine trees

node   joints occurring at intervals along the stem of a plant from which a leaf or bud develops

nutans   nodding, swaying

obtusus   blunt or flattened

octopus style   *tako-zukuri, takozukuri*; exaggeration of informal upright style with many zigs and zags, including rootage and branches

officinalis   medicinal

-oides   like or resembling

omono-**bonsai**   large four-handed bonsai from 30 to 48 inches

opposite   leaf arrangements in pairs along an axis, one opposite the other

organic matter   any material alive at some time, such as peat, bark, and manure

ovate   egg-shaped, with the larger part toward the base

palmate   with leaflets or lobes radiating like outstretched fingers from a central point

parasite   a plant growing on another and using nutrients from the host plant

parvifolius   with small leaves

patens   open, spreading

peeled-bark style   *sharikan*; damage to bark from lightning or other trauma; not driftwood

p'en t'sai   the Chinese word for *bonsai*, an art form predating the Japanese art

perennial   A nonwoody plant that lives for three years or more

perlite   natural minerals expanded by heat to form a light, porous granule for use in propagating or lightening soils

petiole   leaf stalk

phloem   a complex tissue in the vascular system of higher plants consisting mainly of sieve tubes and elongated cells. Its fibers function in translocation, support, and storage

pinching back   nipping of tips of branches by hand

pine-tree shape   *matsu-zukuri*; in the shape of a pine tree; may also be used for deciduous trees

pinnate, pinnatus   a compound leaf with leaflets, usually paired on either side of the stalk like a feather

plenus   double, full

plumosus   feathery

populifolius   with poplar-like leaves

praecox   precocious

procumbens   trailing plant shape

prostratus   prostrate plant shape

pumilus   dwarfish, small plant shape

pungens   piercing

purpureus   purple color

radicans   rooting; especially along the stem

raft style   *ikadabuki*; single tree on its side with branches trained upright as though they were all individual trees; visually creates a forest

repens, reptans   creeping plant shape

reticulatus   net-veined

retusus   notched at blunt apex

rhizome   modified stem which develops horizontally underground

riparius   of river banks

rivalis, rivularis   of brooks

rock-garden style   see *ishizuke, ishitsuke, ishitzuke*

root-connected style   *netsunari*; trees sprout from long surface roots of more than one root stock; occurs naturally in willow, quince, Chinese raintree, vine maple, wild cherry

root-over-rock style   *sekijoju*; tree roots placed over and trained to grow on one or more rocks; trees may be planted immediately in this manner or developed gradually

root stock   part of a grafted plant which supplies the roots; same as understock

roso-zukuri   candle-flame shape; *arborvitae*

rubens, ruber   red, ruddy color

rufus   ruddy color

sabakan   see *hollow-trunk style*

saba-miki, shaba-miki   a bonsai design element that copies natural hollowing and decay of the trunks of hardwood trees; may include the characteristic twisting of the juniper species, the hollowing-out of oak, or the vertical stripping of the trunk in timberline trees as branches die off

saccharatus   sweet, sugary

sagittalis   arrow-like

saikei   a living landscape of trees planted on rocks with streams, cliffs, valleys, and caves, contained in a large flat tray-shaped pot—rock-grown style; multiple trees; multiple rocks; multiple trees and rocks; multiple pots

saikei forest planting   characterized by particular emphasis placed upon a detail, such as trunks, foliage, number of trees, or landscape feature

saikei one tree   placement of one tree next to other elements, such as rock(s), mountain, stream, bush, ridge, mountaintop, cave, natural bridge

saikei two tree   characterized by harmony, balance, interest, and stability of trees and landscape features; similarities in shape, front and back, direction, profile, spacing, position, interval; also, three-tree, five-tree, group planting

salicifolius   with willow-like leaves

sambon-yose   three-tree style; relationship between height, width, branches, and depth symbolic of sun, moon, and earth; heaven, earth, and man; or father, mother, and child

saramiki   *sharimiki*; driftwood style; large areas of dead wood; desert, beach, or high-altitude appearance

saxatilis   inhabiting rocks

scabrus   rough-feeling

scandens   climbing plant shape

scoparius   broom-like

sekijoju root-over-rock; tree placed over and trained to grow on one or more rocks; trees may be planted immediately in this manner or be developed gradually

semicascade style see *han-kengai*; foliage of first branch must extend below top edge of the pot

seven-trunk style *nanahon-yose*; a group planting of seven trees

shakan slanting style with straight or curved trunk; slant is not forward or backwards, and apex not over roots. *Sho-shakan*: minimum slant; *chu-shakan*: medium slant; *dai-shakan*: maximum slant

shari a dead branch or fragment of a dead branch found on hardwood species; found as a horizontal design motif

sharikan peeled-bark style; damage to bark from lightning or other trauma; not driftwood

sharimiki *saramiki*; driftwood style; large areas of dead wood; desert, beach, or high-altitude appearance

shidare-zukuri weeping style; fashioned after the weeping willow tree

shitakusa bulb style; perennials

shito **bonsai** fingertip-size bonsai from 2 to 4 inches

shohin **bonsai** palm-size bonsai from 5 to 8 inches

slanting style *shakan*; straight or curved trunk with slant not forward or backwards and apex not over roots

soju **or** *so-ju* two-tree style; relationship between tree heights, widths, and lowest branches creates illusion of tree in the distance

sokan double-trunk style; two trunks, preferably in the bottom quarter of the tree and one in front of the other

species the word in a botanical name following the genus

sphagnum bog mosses collected as a source of organic soil amendment

split-trunk style *sabamiki*; the trunk of the tree split due to trauma; one side may be dead

spore a simple cell for reproduction in some primitive plants, such as ferns, algae, and moss

sport genetic mutation

sprout style *miyama-kirishima*, *kabudachi*; characterized by sprouts developed on an old stump, a section of fallen tree, or part of a rotten log; sprouts arranged like flowers to contrast new life with old tree

spur specialized short branch on a fruit tree which produces the blossom

stomata microscopically small openings in the epidermis of the green parts of a tree or other plant through which gases pass out of and into the plant from the air

stratification the plant and seed requirement for certain minimum cold periods before successful seed germination or flowering

stress any plant condition that threatens its health, such as too much or too little water

subspecies the word in a botanical name following the genus and species, expressed in lower-case italics, that sometimes precedes the variety or cultivar

sucker plant growth on a grafted plant that originates on the root stock; also improper term for watersprout on fruit trees

suiseki a viewing rock or stone placed on a custom-made, carved, and footed stand to be viewed from a specific perspective

symbiotic describes relationship between two plants in which mutual benefit is derived

systemic any chemical product transported by absorption; the pest at which it is directed is poisoned as it eats its plant "host"

tachiki *moyogi*; informal upright style with curving upright trunk and apex over rootage

takozukuri, *tako-zukuri* octopus style; exaggeration of informal upright style with many zigs and zags, including roots and branches

tama-zukuri ball-shaped

taproot a large, central root that grows fast and straight down to reach a deep water table

tender not hardy; usually genetic, but can refer to plants that need to be hardened off

thinning out pruning to achieve a more open structure in the plant

three-tree style *sambon-yose*; relationship between height, width, branches, and depth symbolic of sun, moon, and earth; heaven, earth, and man; or father, mother, and child

tokonoma   a traditional Japanese display area in the largest room of the home

top dress   to add material, such as mulch or fertilizer, to the surface of the soil

topiary   the art of shaping bushes and trees into unnatural shapes, such as animals or mazes

tosho   triple-trunk style; similar to three-trunk, except all three trunks come from the same tree

truss   a terminal cluster of flowers, such as in the rhododendron genus

tsukami-yose   clustered style; a group style with multiple trunks springing from one tree

twisted style   *nejikan*; trunk spirals upward with growth

two-tree style   *soju, so-ju*; relationship between tree heights, widths, and lowest branches creates illusion of a tree in the distance

umbrella shape   *kasa-zukuri*; in the shape of an umbrella

underplanting   Planting a low plant under a larger one, such as a ground cover under a tall shrub

understock   see *root stock*

variety   also cultivar; any capitalized name in roman letters with single quotation marks; sometimes included in a botanical name, usually following the genus and species (and subspecies, if included), such as *Juniperus chinensis sargentii* 'Shimpaku'.

vermiculite   heat-puffed mica; a soil-lightening amendment

watersprout   unchecked, sudden upward growth as the result of severe pruning

weeping style   *shidare-zukuri*; fashioned after the weeping willow tree

wettable powder   a pesticide that can be applied by first mixing with water

whorl   three or more leaves, branches, or stems growing from one location on a branch; presents a problem in pine bonsai design

windswept style   *fukunigashi*; the slant of the tree indicates wind direction, as though the tree were growing on a mountain or near a beach; slant may be extreme or gentle

yama-yori   fallen-cone style, hundred-tree style; hundreds of sprouts from one vicinity

yatsabusa   plant name designation meaning extremely dwarfed; such plant material generally makes an excellent candidate for saikei

yomayori, yomayose   natural style; natural informal groupings

yose-ue, yose-uye   group planting style; more than nine trees or any larger prime number; a grove or group planting rather than a forest

Bonsai Index

Other Sterling books by Herb L. Gustafson:

The Bonsai Workshop
Keep Your Bonsai Alive & Well
Miniature Living Bonsai Landscapes: The Art of Saikei